My American Dream

My American Dream

Nekemiah Muzazibwa

Rev. date: 06/04/2018

To order additional copies of this book, contact:
Xlibris
1-888-795-4274
www.Xlibris.com
Orders@Xlibris.com
777817

CONTENTS

Preface ix

Chapter 1   My Early Years: Upbringing; Educationiol
Training; Experience Living in a "Foreign Land." 1

Chapter 2   Searching for my Identity: Trips to Africa 16

Chapter 3   Mapping My Future: Pursuing a Graduate
Degree; Adventures in Real Estate Business;
Getting a Reliable Job; Issues on the Social Front 34

Chapter 4   Working in the Real-Estate Business: 2004-2007
– Challenges of Learning the Art of the Industry;
Continuing Poor Health; Problems of Managing
Rental Property and Second Trip to Ghana 58

Chapter 5   Working at a Telecommunication Company,
2007-2011: Benefits and Challengs 69

Chapter 6   A Plunge into the Unknown World:
2011 – Working at Several Companies;
Continuing Social Challenges; Economic
Hardships; Living with MS 97

Chapter 7   Dealing with Realities: Divorce Effects;
Inability to Work; Continued Poor Healthy;
Reflecting on My Life..133

Chapter 8   Concluding Remarks: My Story in a Nutshell,
Lessons Learned..149

Dedication: To My Two Sons

Therapeutic Overview

During My Struggles

PREFACE

Today is November 8th, 2012 which marks the first day I am beginning to write my diary that my parents (Beatrice and Frederick Nkoma) have been encouraging me to work on. Although I thought that this was exciting, I was also somewhat hesitant to embrace the idea on the grounds that I am too young to write my autobiography! However, as time went by, the idea became more inviting, particularly since I felt that I had a duty to explain to my two sons (Peter and Pal) the circumstances that led to my present disability which is multiple sclerosis (MS). What further even became pressing was the fact that as time went by, my disease was making it difficult for me to write down my thoughts. Consequently, I decided that I had to start immediately writing about my life story with the central objective that it may enlighten many people about my struggles with MS, but also it may provide useful experience to many young people as they struggle with various challenges they face in their lives.

CHAPTER 1

My Early Years: Upbringing; Educationiol Training; Experience Living in a "Foreign Land."

I was born in Uganda on February 4, 1974. My other siblings (Arthur Mubiri, Monica Konso, and Olivia Igambi) were also born in Uganda when that country was experiencing political upheavals during Idi Amin's dictatorial rule (1971-1979). In addition to my biological siblings, I have five cousins (Geraldine Nzinga, Emmanuel Mulungi, Dyna Namatede, Fida Namususwa, and Joshua Magezi) who following the deaths of my maternal aunt (Robina) and her husband Jussy Mugweri in 1995 and 1989 respectively, became part of the Nkoma family. Indeed, an outsider will be surprised that all my siblings and cousins have different last names from our parents, but this is due to the naming system in Uganda.

In Uganda, my mother and father were gainfully employed – the former worked as an Administrative Assistant in a government office and the latter was teaching at Uganda's famous university. However, due to political instability, we were forced to flee the country in 1977. Due to my short stay (1974-1977) in Uganda, I have a vague memory of experience of my homeland. I was told that I was sickly as a toddler and almost died from choking while eating peanuts. My health misfortunes did not end here but followed me in the early 1980s when my appendix busted followed with acute pneumonia.

We left Uganda in 1977 when my dad was offered a Fulbright Fellowship to teach at one of the state colleges in Florida. While here, I was diagnosed as a mentally challenged child because I was speaking both my indigenous language Lusoga and English. As it later turned out, much of this was due to ignorance and racism which I am told was rampant in this part of the country. I am told that my mom and my older brother Arthur neutralized the situation by physically "fighting" off all forms of oppression.

Since my dad's job at this university was a one-year appointment (1977-1978), we moved to Minnesota where my dad was offered a tenure-track position as an Assistant Professor at one of the state universities. Our experience here has been a mixed one, involving meeting nice people and running into hard-core racists. Individuals welcomed us warmly. On the other hand, however, one had to deal with everyday American racism involving name calling and pure harassment.

Notwithstanding this fact, I assimilated into the culture where I lived even though I knew my name and language made me distinctly different. I excelled in athletics, like my brother and sisters and this helped me assimilate and make friends. Schooling was easier as achievements in sports helped, but I knew I would have to equally perform in academics. I went to a local elementary school, after which I attended another local junior high, and finally I went to one of the local senior high schools in the area. From kindergarten through 3rd grade, my memories consist of running around and playing games like most kids. But I vividly remember a sound followed by a look of reprimand my mom would give us if we would do something wrong in public places that kept me and my siblings in line. Besides the clicking sound of disdain, nothing would be said with her glares, but interestingly a million words were spoken with just her frown.

We lived in a white house on the north east side of town, which actually was a dangerous and poorer area of town. I made many friends as did my brother and sisters. But it is amazing that trouble was not that common. My mom used to work 10-14 hours a day despite her poor health. My dad would teach non-stop traveling to Ivy League School and to highly respected research university in place. My dad got his tenure and was promoted to a professorship in 1982. Because of my parent's hard work, things began to take shape as my mom finished her Bachelor of Science in Business in 1985. Indeed, their work ethic was contagious for the rest of our family.

Young as I was, I had future dreams such as my mom reuniting with her sister named Robina who she left in Uganda; I also had a dream of going to Africa to see the land and people I only knew via the telephone. Interestingly, in early 1980 my parents started hosting many international students during summer. Most of these students were from Ghana and Uganda. I identified with these people and I loved the communal relationship. I then told my mom that I would marry an African girl.

In 1980 my mom and dad sponsored one of my mom's young sister Mangalita Dhadha to come to the United States. She attended one of the local high schools after which she went to a local state university where she graduated with a Bachelor of Arts in Economics and later on earned her Master's degree in Economics. She was the first family member from Uganda I became acquainted with on a face to face basis. This experience was encouraging to me as I could see the fruits of my parent's labor paying off. I knew from seeing this, that if I put my mind to something I could do the same. Some years later my parents sponsored my Uncle Milton Kutegana to come and study at a local state university pursuing his Master's degree in English and his younger brother, Uncle Noah Ivule who studied Computer Science at a local technical college.

After Aunt Mangalita joined the family and us children getting big, the house we lived in became small to accommodate us all. My parents decided to move to a bigger house and in a better area of town. This house had a yellow siding so we called this house "the yellow house". This became the home where my long lasting personal and young adult life started. As a youth, I tried to work many different jobs at a time which was inefficient and an overkill from a cost-effective perspective, but the drive to always be in motion and working was inherited from my parents. Although my physical health will not allow me to work today like I once did, I still think constantly of my next 'gig' or assignment where I will make my next hundreds, thousands and millions. To get my millions, I knew at an early age that academics would have to be my niche as that is what allowed my family to establish our name in our community. I worked very hard to excel in athletics, but I found myself losing focus in my academics. There was a lot of politics both in athletics and academics. I would find myself getting depressed and hoping that maybe I will have an intervention from God in the form of putting 65 to 70 pounds of muscles on my body and growing at least to 6 feet and 6 inches like Michael Jordan. I would watch his documentary 'Come fly with me' non-stop as a boy and shot baskets outside in the cold in hopes of improving my jump shots. Although I excelled at Soccer, I was greatly disturbed that I was not getting the same breakthrough in basketball. My social life was compromised because of my attention to basketball and so I started dancing to express myself. Rhythms came natural and I was skinny and flexible. In other words, I was a good dancer! People who knew me, knew I could get down and I enjoyed this distinction as it somewhat set me apart from my siblings. In fact, because of my creativity in dancing, I was invited, with some dance partners to participate in my high school jamboree which was a forum to showcase the group talent. We won this contest which I think introduced a dancing fad. In spite of my popularity on the dancing front, I was experiencing rebellion and self-loathing as an adolescent. It was 1987 at a local junior high when changes began to happen in my body and my life. Dancing, music, girls and sports became my life. I would have private times when I would think and reflect, but I wanted to be popular and accepted by the 'in crowd.'

With all the positives I had going, I sometimes thought I could do whatever I wanted without any repercussions. However, I got a rude of awakening when I shop lifted and got into trouble and my parents had to come to my rescue. This was unfortunate because they had a lot of issues raising us four children in a foreign land to begin with; but this left them wondering if they had done some something wrong with me especially since I am a middle child. I believe in hindsight, my parents knew that I was their eccentric son, who would either become something very special or very sad and that left them keeping a close eye on my activities, as our American story was still unfolding.

It was good that my brother and sisters were very competitive both academically and athletically. This helped me realize that each of us were dealing with racial issues in our own ways. As a male, I could relate closely with my brother's struggle even though my younger sister, Olivia's episodes were closer to mine since we are very close in age and we went to the same schools. My older sister Monica and I would speak about our plans to make millions and always wondered who would accomplish this first. With the resistance all of us four children encountered in high school, and with college approaching, our oldest brother led the charge by working very hard and as a result got accepted to a local private college in Minnesota. He could have chosen to go to a local state university, but he decided against that scenario because he was also offered a partial athletic scholarship by this private college. In hindsight, I do not think my parents realized that this was only a one-year scholarship when they allowed him to join this college. But he later joined the ROTC to help finance his education. He really set the precedent for the rest of us.

My older sister Monica also chose to go to a private college north of the state. But as my turn was approaching, the decision was not as clear cut as my siblings because even though I had matured much, my recent run ins with the law and volatile health past brought much scrutiny to my decision. After seeing my older brother and sister making it to private schools, I decided that I would have to prove myself academically and that would require me forfeiting my aspirations in basketball because it was consuming too much of my time and energy which compromised my academics. On October 31, 1991, of my senior year, which was coincidentally Halloween, I experienced something which provided impetus for my decision not to play basketball. A fellow student (whom I thought was a friend) called me a 'nigger'. Unlike my older brother, I reacted to this incident not initially with my fists, but with words in response as pain, emotions, and confusion were running through me at the time. Many of my 'friends' at that time were also my brother's friends too but after this incident, I was not sure if they were really my friends. I, also knew that if my academics were further compromised because of basketball I would become the only one of my siblings not to go to a private school. This was further exacerbated my emotions of being called the "n" word by a so called 'friend'.

I did not announce the departure from the game I loved dearly because I continued to go to try outs and made the team and I know my coaches were impressed with my game and the 25+ pounds of muscle I added to my skinny frame. It was not until my coach referred to me as Mubiri (my older brother) that I vividly remembered the foolish head games that "coaches" and so called "friends" were playing with me. At this point, I decided to announce that I was not going to play my senior year because the game I loved was not fun for me anymore. Coming clean with my coach gave me the confidence I needed to step out and make a name for myself in many other ways. I wondered for some time if I made the right decision not to play basketball in my senior year of high school. This decision tormented me for some time but in long run it paid off, because I managed to divert my energies into other activities I enjoyed doing such as dancing which interestingly was an artistic expression of what was going on in my life.

I would go to local spots while managing my academics and bringing my grade point average up to a 3.75 in my senior year. As I was enjoying my adolescent maturity and creativity, two events took place that took me aback: 1) my academic 'counselor' looked at my past year's grades, called me into his office and he told me I would never make it into a good private university like my brother and sister did. He went on to suggest that maybe I should settle for a vocational school; 2) the local newspaper had an article about gang problems in the city and put my picture by the article which implied that I was part of the gang. These two events gave me much motivation to succeed and go to a private college. Indeed, these events also brought a new dimension into my lifeline. I was now more determined than before to see that I perform very well academically and achieve this goal.

I was interested in a few private liberal arts colleges in the midwest states. I visited one of them in Iowa and I really liked it. It was beautiful and I knew I would be in the same school and maybe even be roommate with one of my good high school friends. The only problem with this school was that it was in the middle of nowhere. Despite the attractions these schools had, I decided to attend a private college which was near home. Besides, my parents were not too comfortable allowing me to go that far given my healthy issues and the recent behavior I had displayed. Although I chose a school which is near home, still my parents were very hesitant to let me go and stay away on campus. After a long discussion, they told me that I would have to commute the first year after which they will let me go and live on campus after I prove that I was serious about school. In hindsight, I believe this was a good decision they made for me.

During this first year I made some notable academic achievements which included being able to articulate myself both orally and in writing. I wrote several lengthy papers from which the general feedback from the professors was good. This increased my confidence. I specifically remember in my American history class when the professor had us write a paper on a documentary named 'Glory' which was about a black infantry that fought but was defeated in a battle during the Civil War. I remember the passion I had as I wrote my paper and as an 18-year old boy just coming out of high school. I was able to coherently articulate my thoughts of the racist ulterior motives of the north in sending a black battalion to fight a battle in which so many human lives would most probably be lost. I remember my instructors astounding comments on this paper, not for just how well it read, but the idea that perhaps a black battalion was sent to this battle because they knew human fatality would be significant; I got an 'A' in the class. He further made astounding remarks and gave me a word of encouragement. All in all, at the end of my first year in college, I managed to achieve a 3.5 GPA which boosted my self-confidence and I now knew that despite what anybody else may do or say, I could achieve anything I wanted academically as well as athletically, if I put my mind to it.

In addition to excelling in academics, I also made new friends both from school and in the community that to this day invoke some very sweet memories. With these new friends, I would go out partying and dancing showing my creativity that I discovered in high school. Some of these new friends came from south side of Chicago. I could not relate to the streets they were from, but I could relate to their soul music. Always remember dancing is a language being spoken on the dance floor that was both articulated in the music and the dance. As scripture states in Ecclesiastes 1:9, 'there is no new thing under the sun' and I learned that music, dances, customs, exercises and even martial arts are a means of expression that have been done before.

With that being said, the opportunity was still there for me to try out for the university team for both basketball and soccer. I kept playing intramural basketball and picked up soccer with friends but in spite of how good all this was, my high school experience and the mental torture I felt plus the politics deterred me from pursuing this sport on a collegiate level. However, I had mixed feelings about the help my older brother Arthur gave me about soccer. On the one hand, I appreciated the excellent soccer help he introduced me to, but on the other hand I did not like the fact that my performance was overshadowed by his excellent record. Nonetheless, I knew this was my time and with tryouts winding down and moving on to campus, I was ready to start this era of my life.

I stopped commuting and moved into the dorm starting my second year. At this time my younger sister was going to join a private college in south Minnesota which is 100 miles away from home while my older sister was completing her first degree. Around the same time Aunt Mangalita had completed her Master's degree, got married and moved to the East Coast. After a year, Uncle Milton also moved on to one of the state universities in Arizona to purse his Ph D.. My parents were now living in an empty nest. This was indeed a different way of life for my parents after all those years of having a large family at home.

After I moved into the dorm, I soon realized the complexity of living with other people and not having my own personal space. I did not like my roommate because he was smoking and sometime acted strange. It was always very difficult to study or even have any academic discussion with him. We ended up splitting and he found another place to stay. After he moved out, I was able to pick up from where I stopped in my fresh man year and focused on my academics.

My college life on campus began to develop a unique experience. I started enjoying philosophy and business classes more than other subjects. I felt that my speaking, thinking, reasoning, and writing became clearer and more persuasive than before. At this point, studying law crossed my mind as a future possibility but I did not give it too much thought at this particular moment. Although I enjoyed studying Philosophy very much, it did not give me the complete answers I was looking for. However, Political Science, seemed to be a better alternative for me. The external pressure to make a decision for what I wanted to be for the rest of my life was mounting.

On a personal front, things were still complex in my own life since my African roots were becoming more removed. My situation worsened when I became a member of the student senate which had both positive and negative effects on me. For example, my senate responsibility somewhat impeded my main goal of finding out more about my "motherland continent Africa." Part of this desire arose out of my minimum understanding of Africa which involved: wearing African clothes; eating African foods; speaking my mother tongue (Lusoga); and like African Americans getting superficial knowledge from the "Discovery Channels". At the end of the day, I was in a personal predicament which entailed not knowing when my time would come that I would see Africa again and get more educated. The more I would speak about it with other students the more 'homesick' I would become over a land I never really knew because all my understanding was based on stories from my mom and dad that were becoming less and less personal and more word of mouth (because of my age when my family fled to the United States). Since I also got involved in the wrong crowd at school, I needed to stay in an organization that would keep me involved in a positive way. Furthermore, things were still complex in my own life as a result of a bicycle accident that resulted in breaking my hand, forcing me to use my left hand while writing. The damages to my body were obvious and I was in pain. Thus I immediately contacted an attorney and briefed him about my accident. The monetary recovery I got from the lawsuit helped me finance my trips to Africa.

Coincidently, as I was struggling with the issue of identity, an organization known as the "Black Man's Think Tank" was started which focused on examining pressing issues facing black students. This organization provided a forum to discuss not only challenges facing blacks in the USA, but also highlighted issues relating to blacks elsewhere. This came about as a result of the two local private universities began recruiting more international students. Interestingly, the man who created this group was an eccentric well educated white man.

But at this time, which was around December of 1993, I realized that I would need to get myself a steady girlfriend as I needed someone to talk to and share time with instead of random flings as I was accustomed to. In an unorthodox fashion, I therefore started dating/talking to girls online which was new, mystical, intriguing and exotic as well as different. I believe this is a trait that would identify the kind of person I was. It seemed, furthermore, that the only girls at a private college nearby that I knew were only interested in the party scene, which I still was in to, but I wanted more of a personal connection than that. However, I also found myself becoming more and more of an introvert as things were becoming more demanding in my life. It was at this time nevertheless, that I obtained my U.S. citizenship which was important for me for my future endeavors.

Since I left school soccer, I was at this time disconnected from that group. I began to find solace in thinking as I thought philosophy was my natural calling. I could not find any answers in this area, but it gave me a sense of 'liberty', especially since I started to understand the writings of Nietzsche, Heidegger, Levinas, Plato, Socrates and other major thinkers in philosophy and psychology. I was not finding answers with these writers, however, but my reasoning, thinking and writing were greatly improved. I was still lonely though and I would express my general disdain for my situation through music. I listened to everything, but a lot of gangster rap. I was blessed growing up in an educated middle-class household once again and so I could not relate to the street roots of the music, but I could relate to the general rage.

In the midst of the drama of the student senate, school and lack of a consistent girlfriend, I found my determinations to make it through this situation even greater. I believe these situations made me into the lone type of ranger that I am now. I could relate to a lot of different kinds of people and I could only relate to many of my college roommates on a superficial level. For example, I had an eccentric roommate who was annoying. He had ADHD, which I think, he used to his advantage to gain sympathy from people or instructors but I cynically thought he could control some of his behavior he showed.

I knew I needed a hustle of some sort, but things were difficult for me at this stage because I was making minimal money at my work-study job at the computer lab. Computer science was rapidly gaining demand on the market, but my older brother chose this area which turned me off as an authentic area for me. All I could was hope that an opportunity would open up that would become 'authentically' mine.

In the interim, I was finishing up my junior year of college and I was beat up emotionally and physically, from my participation in the student senate as I grew cynical of people whom I thought were my friends, but turned a cold shoulder when I needed them. Thus I learned to become a shady loner; it is around this time that I started a smoking habit mixed with chewing tobacco that was nasty and unhealthy. I did, however, have some consolation in participating in the Black Man's Think Tank.

Things changed for me as my 21st birthday was approaching. Like everyone else I knew, I was a drinker and partier, but the thrill of doing all this illegally as a minor was subsiding as many of my contemporaries had already become of age. Furthermore, my maturity had transformed substantially as serious thoughts of what I would do for a career were in the forefront of my mind, and my student loans were piling up too. On a personal front, I thought of myself as an attorney or professor of philosophy or something; but, I had not seen the country or continent of my birth which left a tremendous void in me, nonetheless. Also, my health had deteriorated as I had put weight on from my lack of involvement in athletics, coupled with the aforementioned habits that were only making things worse.

I set a mark for myself, which consisted of transforming my physical health and bringing my body back to the superb physical condition I was in back when I was training for soccer tryouts years back. To begin with, I started lifting weights again, but with the weight I had put on coupled with the smoking habit made achieving my goal difficult as I was sensitive and cynical to criticism from others as I wanted this to be a personal matter. I was seeing only a little progress, but not as quickly as I wanted; indeed, this was evidence of the harm I had done to my body. But nonetheless, I evaluated my progress based on how I felt.

I started swimming as part of my exercise, coupled with playing basketball and lifting weights, the transformation became more apparent. Also, I started to eat healthy foods and people began to recognize what a specimen I was becoming. Additionally, clothes began to fit me better, as well. In fact, I created a wardrobe that was uniquely me.

As my time in college was coming to an end, I was determined to go out with a bang! Not only was I making exercise a necessity, but I needed to make dancing my trademark as that was my style. Dancing and exercising were distancing me from the demons that I allowed to creep into my life (all the smoking and chewing tobacco). I had roommates my senior year that were still reminding me and bringing me down as they had an impression of me that was from my junior year where I was in pain psychologically with my student senate experience and physically with my aforementioned habits and the weight I had gained; as with the other demons of my junior year, I severed these ties, and we went our ways half way through my senior year, which was a huge blessing for me. At this point, I got a native American roommate named Steve who became one of my dearest friends, to date.

I intensified my working out and regained my social life. I believe because the impetus for this was the positivity I had with my living arrangements. Steve and I were like brothers kind of like how Chris and I were my freshman year. The difference was Steve was from a well to do middle class family as I was. Unlike myself, he looked white and he spoke like a white American kid as I did. I liked how he was emphatic that he was native American Ojibwe as I was too as an African from Uganda. This friendship made me feel void, nevertheless, as I could only claim African roots, but my cognitive memory of Uganda was distant from me.

Nonetheless, we would joke non-stop about things that were serious on the greater scheme of things such as issues like racism or bigotry. This was therapeutic to me. We would also party which made our college experience more fun and educational too. Additionally, we both listened to similar music from Tupac (rap) to Rage Against the Machine (alternative rock). We also took some classes together, many of which we would just laugh our way through. One of the classes we took was African History which actually had a very serious undertone for me, as that was my dad's specialty. Even though I felt the class lacked structure, the Professor himself would be pivotal for what was next to transpire in my life.

Notwithstanding these events, my transformation involved with my healthy living and social life were evident. I added swimming to my repertoire and the physical changes were evident as I began to look like a model. In addition to my regiment I rediscovered that a wholesome smile and laughter were healthy, as well, and these did a lot for me. Also, I got my 'step' back on the dance floor, which further mesmerized the masses. In fact, I made dancing a regular part of my weekly, if not daily, regiment.

In the spring of 1996, as my graduation was nearing, I realized just how much I had changed since I started college. Also, all of my self-introspection also made the reality that now I had to choose a career perspective as I would need a job or show a sign to someone, especially me, as to what my next step would be. I, therefore, applied to law schools thinking that was my calling. I received several denial letters, but that gave me more motivation to keep applying, which I did. At the same time, I missed all of the job fairs in a thriving economy and I walked through my graduation ceremony. I thought about joining the United States Marines as I was deeply fascinated with the discipline and structure of that institution. But I was very much an intellect and I wanted to pursue more academia at the same time.

Thus, I decided that my only option after I graduated was to live at home, find a full-time job and to keep applying to law schools. Unfortunately, I was getting denial letters one after another and my confidence and self-pride was diminishing; but, at the last moment, I received a conditional acceptance letter from one of law colleges in cities which allowed me to pick up my head after struggling and obtaining my college degree from a private school.

My mind was set on obtaining my law degree from this University which is in about 65-70 miles away from home. There was a condition that I take a course at here for eight weeks before I could be fully accepted in their program. There was an upfront cost, but I believe my earlier problems with the law inhibited mom and dad from allowing me to go and live on campus for this course. I still had that overcoming spirit in me, nonetheless, and I commuted to campus to take the course. I would discover that the courses were mostly discussion and reading a lot of cases. Since I was in excellent physical health, I did not mind the daily grind starting at 5:30 AM each morning, but the case examinations would make my days long and I found I had little time for out of classroom discussion on cases or even socializing with other students and I was too tired to exercise daily to keep my body healthy after driving home. Subsequently, I found myself a step behind, compared to my classmates. I, however, did take away some lifelong valuable legal principles.

At the end of the day, I found myself back at mom and dad's and I started my first full time job in bill collections. I felt somewhat accomplished as I had finished college, gone to law school of some sort, but going back to Africa, was not accomplished. It was around October of 1996, nonetheless, that I received a phone call from a Law Firm which I had contacted when I broke my arm from the bicycle accident years before. The caller told me that the settlement from the accident was approved and that I needed to meet with the other party.

I did not know what to do or say when I met with the other parties' attorney, but I did understand that they were going to write me a check. When their attorney met with me, he asked me in a flattering manner 'how much do you bench-press'? He asked me this because I looked healthy and rehabilitated from any broken arm. Not knowing he was appealing to my ego, I proudly answered 350lbs. I did not say anything about how I was still having pain and discomfort resonating in my arm after I broke it. In general, I did not want to give out details that would mess up my settlement. Nonetheless, his 'trick' worked and we settled for only $10,000, even though I could have easily recovered much more than what was offered to me. Nonetheless, I felt some closure and I was content because this matter was fairly adjudicated. I was also grateful that I spoke with this attorney after my accident who helped me get compensated for the negligence of the defective bicycle that I purchased. At the end of the day, I used some of the proceeds as a down payment on my first vehicle, which was a 1995 Mazda 626 which was hot! I also had funds remaining that I saved.

CHAPTER 2

Searching for my Identity: Trips to Africa

Soon after my accident settlement, I received a call from mu undergraduate college inviting me to participate in a trip to Ghana the school was planning for its students. I was working full time and my emotions were sporadic as I did not know how to respond at first. But time was of the essence and when I ran this proposition past my mom and dad, they immediately responded with an emphatic 'yes', as we had many lifelong friends from Ghana

I began my planning for my trip and continued with my day to day post college life. On a domestic front in the states, I continued to make friends and reach out to different opportunities and I found myself gravitating towards the African student plight here in the US.

It was at this time before my trip that I met a clique of Africans from West Africa, Ethiopia, and America who lived in a house by a local state university that liked to party. There was a guy from Guinea, West Africa another one was from Sierra Leone, West Africa, and one from Ethiopia. These guys were the ringleaders and became my crew including another eccentric person I met named 'Smart', who was an intelligent, fast money and street smart person and there was a black American as well. Honestly, the friendship and memories from this crew that I established were stronger than those from any group I ever had at any time in my life. I am grateful for each and every one of them as the timing was perfect in my life.

The celebrating, moreover, was weekends, starting Wednesdays through Sundays would be party time some not ending till 6am in the morning. I met many African students from the diaspora and we would party nights away. It is at this point that the African in me was resurrected. I would socialize and talk politics and felt like I was truly going to change Africa as I would talk politics, ideas and plans for wealth with the other African students was always the focal point. I believed this would become a reality as I was preparing to travel to Ghana in the next couple of weeks.

At this time, I met individuals that would touch my life in a way others had not up to this point. First, there was a girl from Eritrea that I met with a young baby girl. She was eccentric and funny, and I became close friends with her. We would kiss often, go dancing and once in a while we would go to professional basketball games sometimes with courtside seats with VIP treatment. I was really liking her, but my over thinking, which was too analytical, told me not to pursue her at this time because she had baggage with unresolved issues with her babies' dad. I was looking for and found a girl I could love but I did not listen to my gut feelings to pursue her despite what I felt in my heart; I think she felt the same way about me, too. She is a special girl and to me will always have a special place in my heart.

I thought that perhaps my trip to Africa would resolve and settle my feelings of emptiness as that is my continent of birth. Fortunately, that is what was on deck for me as the final days before my departure were approaching. On the day of my departure, my dad drove me to the drop off where I was meeting with the rest of the group. I vividly remember the somber look on his face when I was 'officially' leaving for Ghana. We had numerous lifelong friends from Ghana and one of them gave me a brown kango that would become my trademark hat during my trip in Ghana and among my peers here in the states.

The plane was off and running and Amsterdam was our first stop as Ghana was our final destination. To be honest, I was not fond of many of the other students I was traveling with. I must admit that the Netherlands had a very pleasant vibe when we arrived at the airport. Quickly we were off and flying to Accra, Ghana. As we approached

Kotoka airport in Ghana, I noticed several people stood up on the plane and began shaking hands. They began to say 'Akwaba' which means welcome in the Twi language of Ghana. This was common as I noticed people would say this at the airport too and at the marketplace where I would shop for memorabilia. The people were welcoming and that calmed my nerves this being this far away from home. It was not obvious that I was a visitor as everyone was dark like me.

At first, I have to admit that I did not like Ghana because of the humidity during the day and our luggage was delayed at Amsterdam, while at the same time we also had mechanical problems at our housing quarters as the water was not running. In addition to no change of clothes, I felt like these two and half weeks would be a punishment. I was so used to the good life in the states that I could not see the practicality of adjusting to conditions in Ghana.

After a while though, I began to forget the 9 to 5 structure of my life, and I began to observe how beautiful things actually were in Ghana. The people did not have a 'Minnesota nice' often fake-ness about them, but simplicity and genuine appreciation for life and people is what I began to notice. For example, an Uncle of one of the Ghanaian students I knew as parents hosted him back home in the USA came and picked me up and took me out to eat at Shangri-La restaurant. I felt loved and welcomed in Ghana because of this gesture. I also developed a liking for fufu, which is a Ghanaian or West African delicacy. This inviting action would set the stage for me for what was to further transpire in Ghana and back in Minnesota as I would become close friends with his son who went to school in Minnesota and later purchase my home from his nephew too.

My inhibitions, furthermore, began to come down as I realized how much of a defense I had put up in my years leading up to this Ghana trip as I was raised and lived in a predominantly white environment up till then in the states. Coincidently, some of the first people I became friends with were white students from California who were on a one year study abroad. Interestingly, they were fluent in Twi, which is the language of the Ashanti people and spoken through much of Ghana. Notwithstanding this fact however, I did not feel like people were watching me nonstop just because I am black, but I began to see things differently. I enjoyed this freedom as we went to the market and I would shop for memorabilia and stuff I would bring back to the states. I connected with the locals and I felt a lot of compassion for the young boarding school students and they got close to me too. We took pictures. I could see they were poor, and so I gave them money and I would tell them to study and remember my name, which they in unison they would yell Nekemiah!

These kids were not mine (even though I adopted them into my spiritual life), and so I began to think of them like they were, as I thought of starting a philanthropic orphanage and calling it the "Nekemiah's Empire". I do not think these children were orphans, but my ideas were developed as these children melted my heart one after another in that they would ask me for pens so they could write me letters and become my pen-pal. This made me realize how blessed we are in the states and how I wanted to make a lot of money so I could keep them schooled, fed and properly clothed. None of them were beggars and they did not try to steal from me as they knew I was from the states. This deepened my love for the Ghanaian people, coupled with the sight-seeing we were experiencing, like visiting the Elmina and Cape Coast slave castles and the Nkrumah circle. Only time and space would limit what I could buy or give away.

Activities would intensify as we would travel from one historic site to another. One day we were at the University of Ghana dance school and we saw students perform from there and then we went to Koko Beta beach. It was scenic as the tides would flow onto the beach. I am not a surfer but I enjoy the water so I went swimming. This was an incredible and nearly fatal act! To begin with, I let the water from the tide engulf me as I was breathing when the tide would rise. Finally, the tide stopped and I was swimming toward the abyss in the ocean. I probably was in 200+ yards of water. I was an excellent swimmer, but I realized I might have swam too far into the ocean because I lost sight of the horizon when I stopped and looked back. No one could see me and could not see them either. There was an ocean in every direction. I was missing for over thirty minutes in the ocean. Even though I was an excellent swimmer and healthy, I still could have easily panicked, which I think would have invited unwanted predators like sharks because the ocean is full of them. Secondly, I could have lost my sense of direction because I could not see the horizon and therefore turned and swam the wrong way taking me further into the deep ocean. Thus, my life story would have ended there. But I found the tides as I causally swam back and floated my way back to shore guiding the waves with my body the closer I got. I reached dry ground about 100 meters down from where I entered. Words cannot fully describe the look on my peers' faces, who were speaking with the beach manager as I walked up to them on shore. Again, I did not return at the same place I went in ad s o I walked back to them from down at the beach. They most probably thought I was dead in the waters, abducted or lost as there was no account for me for more than thirty minutes! I was calm throughout, nonetheless.

Another occurrence at Koko Beta Beach that happened to me was meeting this guy at the beach who was from Eritrea and who happened to attend a local state university. We only saw each other as strangers in Ghana. Indeed, we would later become good friends at the university. Interestingly, I would later also meet his dad the following year in Uganda as he worked for the United Nations which is what brought him to Ghana. Again, I only realized who he was and became friends with him and his elder sister after I got back to my home town. They were also close to the girl with a little baby that I was getting very close with there too. Nonetheless, my disappearing act in the ocean and meeting my friend from Eritrea all transpired in Ghana and contributed more to my unique Ghana experience 1997.

Activities and events would continue to become more event filled as we travelled to the Chief's palace in Kumasi and hear stories about Osei-Tutu, Nana Prempeh II and Yaa Asantewaa. The latter was a woman who fought off the British and defended the 'Golden Stool' within the Chiefs palace. I soon learned that the 'Golden Stool' is sacred among the Ashanti people, but also has an intrinsic and highly substantive gold value. Nonetheless, the Chief's palace, as with other places, was very well maintained. The people were welcoming and I found out that Kumasi was the heart of the home of the Ashanti people and the Twi language. We would tour more historic places in Ghana like the Kakum National rain forest, which is one of the eight wonders of the world.

As part of our tourism, we would also go to the nightclubs. It was my experience in Ghana's nightlife, however, where I dangerously showed off my individuality. Specifically, one night at Glen's nightclub, I was dancing and enjoying myself and the environment while my peers were getting themselves inebriated, like most other nights. Indeed, we were all in college or recently graduated and so this type of behavior was the norm. But since I recently had just experienced some profound events, which I previously eluded to, I was looking at this night on more of a spiritual level. As the night went by, I found myself dancing, socializing and meeting the local people as my peers drank the evening away. As his was happening, there was a girl who caught my attention that I was flirting with and she seemed to be there with a guy. Before I knew it, however, my peers that I had come with, were all gone! They must have collectively decided that they needed to call it a night. Perhaps they also thought that I knew where we were staying as I was comfortably assimilated with the local people and not hanging out with them.

It was dark and late. I needed to go home. But, where was home? I started to panic as I thought of what could happen to me. There were taxis everywhere, but where do I tell them to drive to? I approached one of the locals named Peter, who was with that girl, and told him that I was looking for my friends and I was not sure where I was staying. He understood me and my American English and called a taxi. I did not know where I was sleeping and the local guy, along with a taxi driver drove me around for up to two hours in pitch black darkness looking for my residence as they spoke an unknown language to me. Truly I have never felt so scared or helpless in my life than I did this night. I had all my money on me and I thought I was most probably a dead man! Out of desperation, I kept saying I work for the US government because I wanted them to know that I am not to be messed with.

I finally recognized a restaurant we were staying at and the cab driver woke up the owner. They spoke to him in an unknown tongue to me, and the owner agreed that I could stay at his restaurant and sleep on the table, if I wanted. As I stepped outside the car I was still nervous thinking they would ambush me. I was ready for a fist fight even though I was outnumbered, but the local guy, the cab driver, and the restaurant owner did not gang up on me to take my money! They wanted to make sure I was safe. Indeed the cab driver asked for a modest fee for all his driving because that was his livelihood but the local guy named Peter did not want money.

I spent the night resting on the hard wood table and I wanted my comfortable bed. I rose up early and started walking towards where I thought we were staying. I almost got lost again so I began taking pictures with my camera of the ground where I thought I would die for sure. A local man, named Musah, who was staying at our quarters saw me walking alone and he picked me up and gave me a ride home. I amazingly made it back to our quarters the next morning alive! As I approached the group I came with they looked at me in awe as they realized I had not spent the night at our quarters. They probably thought I was a ghost as I walked up to them as they were taking head counts to leave for breakfast and no words were exchanged with me because I needed rest.

This night was just crazy as I slept throughout the day. I caught up with me the group after I had awoke and readied myself for the day's/ evenings activities. As I reflected on the previous day's events, I realized nobody, but me, knew what had just happened to me that night, much like my disappearance in the ocean at Koko Beta Beach. In hindsight I realize that God sent his angels at both occurrences to protect me and make sure I was safe. With regard to the events at the nightclub and my journey home, I found out that the guy named Peter who escorted me at night had a reputation as a womanizer as he also became my friend. He would stop by to chill out at our residence as he discovered that we were all tourists from America. He also was a very good dancer and one night at a club there was that same girl he brought with him who also was a good dancer. I knew she was Ghanaian or West African based from her appearance. This night, however, I saw something amazing when I looked in her eyes and she looked in mine; I saw a glimpse of my unborn children coming through her. This was the deepest impression of an angelic touch that I had never experienced. I did not really know this girl, but the impression was deep and very peaceful. The thought of marrying an African woman I spoke out loud to my mom as a child came back to me when I met this girl. This vision was probably the most vivid and profound I had ever had in my life. I studied her actions and movements on the dance floor at Labody Beach and I also liked what I saw; but I was meeting her in a night club in Africa! Even though I had a lot of rhythm and we meshed well on the dance floor, I knew that this was no place to meet my future bride and mother or my children. Additionally, I knew my stay there would be only temporary.

Nonetheless, I continued with my studying her and the nightclub was the only place I could talk to her as a majority of our time began just going there as we would dance to Foxy Brown's remake with Blackstreet 'Take me home' along with Mark Morrison's 'Return of the Mack' as if the music was about us; but the words coincidently in both these songs would be descriptive of what would transpire between us in the future in an odd way.

One beautiful night in Accra as we were dancing at Labody beach, we went away for a walk on the beach and we began holding hands and kissing. I had no fear of getting separated from my group as I knew where I was staying. Not only did I now know where we were staying, but I naively trusted that no-one would harm me, either. Eventually, all my time was being spent with her as she gave me her phone number and she came home with me and we spent the night together. My roommate could detect the chemistry when I brought her home, and so he stepped out of the room.

Everything happens for a reason, but I could not discern the magnitude of what transpired to me as we were nearing the end of our trip. Indeed, Ghana was an amazing two and half weeks and I could tell everyone else was equally as impressed. But my Koko Beta Beach and Glenn's disappearing acts were now my unique story. When the guy, who was my escort when I was looking for my home, named Peter, knew we were soon to depart, he handed me a Ghanaian CD (currency) with a picture of Yasantewa, who looked exactly like that girl I met. I was yet unsure, nonetheless what I would pursue next in my life, but I was thinking something academic at the University of Ghana after what transpired for me there. Frankly, I did not want to leave, but our brief stay was coming to an end.

Our departure was smooth, we were now accustomed to the heat, but it was freezing in Minnesota. Our layover in Amsterdam gave us a heads-up to how cold it was going to get when we got home. Interestingly, I adjusted fine, but the substantive memories were significant. Namely, it was the people, the market-place, the music and that girl I met that made me miss Ghana more and more. In fact, it was difficult to hear the songs on the radio because I would dance without my friends that I made in Accra there with me. Coupled with the marketplace and people I was getting homesick even though Ghana was not my natural place of birth. Additionally, I was receiving letters from the children I had met in Accra that made me feel that they missed me too.

As I was looking at pictures and going through stuff, I ran across the phone number that the girl I met gave me. Since I had a phone in my room, I would call her often. Although her English was limited, as soon as she found out that I lived in the states she started to pay close attention in order to understand what I was saying. We would exchange information about each other, such as likes and dislikes. When I told her my birthday, she then said hers was 'coincidentally' on the same day as mine. Indeed, I met other women afterwards, as well, but I did miss her and I wanted to see her again and so I prayed that God would make a way. Strangely, as this was going on, my relationship with the Eritrean girl lessened.

At this time, I would continue with my 9 to 5 grind as my thoughts of law school or even criminology became less and less of what I wanted to pursue. After seeing the hustle of people in Accra, I knew I wanted to start my own hustle of some sort. But to stick to my guns, I would continue applying to law schools and talking the talk. But my life at this point, nonetheless, took on a noticeably different direction. I had a glow on my face as Ghana changed my demeanor. My work life took on a deeper meaning after what I had seen in Ghana and helping the people I wanted to help would require much hard work, and a lot of it on my part. Good thing my parents set the bar required for hard work for me and my family, as I previously mentioned.

I did not take any time off work after my return and when I was a few weeks back from Ghana, I started to get sick from something. I began to vomit and throw up profusely and my weight began to drop rapidly. I was in excellent physical condition, but this sickness took me out and I was admitted to the hospital. The nurses and a specialist doctor in infectious disease, were dumbfounded at what my sickness was. They were running nonstop blood tests, ran a few CT scans and made sure I was hydrated, but they could not quite put a finger on what I had. There was also an unusual nagging in my body occasionally, but I was still in pristine physical condition as I seemed to self-heal within a few days in the hospital. I didn't want to be on my back in the hospital as they ran nonstop test but with no answers. I began to constantly ask what they found, which I suspected was nothing specific. I felt strong again and restless and they released me.

After I got discharged, I was still running five miles a day in about five minutes per mile increments while playing soccer and basketball and I could bench-press around 400 pounds. This medical anomaly, nonetheless, became another chapter in my medical mishaps that I previously eluded to and I realized how these well-educated doctors have a self-pride and God complex meaning that if they could not figure it out, then no one can as I don't think my ailment was diagnosed.

This medical mystery would become part of my Ghanaian trip experience and my uniqueness as I attributed the cause of my sickness to my disappearing act when I was swimming in the Atlantic Ocean at Koko Beta beach in Ghana. Interestingly I do not think the doctor knew what I had and so that worked for him.

I soon met a number of people who consoled me after I got back from Ghana. First, I met the son of the man who picked me up in Accra. Also I met a pretty Ghanaian girl with a touch of Arab blood and mysticism that I liked that was friends with him. I got close to her and we would go dancing and had some nice private moments. Secondly, I met a girl from Uganda who I like and whose family is well known in the Twin Cities Ugandan community. I also met a group of students from one of the universities in the cities and another group from a local state college here in town. My bond grew closer with these friends since they were young Africans, like me, and they liked to party and talk politics and girls, as I did.

Interestingly, I also met this white guy around this time named Dave, who was a real estate agent and seemingly a likeable guy who knew how to hustle for his money. One night as I was at his house near downtown he began to explain how he owned six homes which, at that time, did not make any sense to me, until I realized what he was doing with these houses and how he was making money from them. This evening when I met him would set the stage for the next several years in my life, both academically as I decided an MBA would be what I would pursue academically and financially in real estate. Meeting Dave was important in my personal life as his advice about real estate investments was financially timely for a variety of ventures I later got into.

Things began to take shape and got focused for me in so far as my introduction to Dave, coupled with thoughts of the hustle I witnessed in Ghana and becoming friends with a Ghanaian and Kenyan in town and seeing their business 'African Enterprise' do well was giving me thoughts of making my millions in the hustle too.

As I became more involved with the Student Association, I learned that there was a very affluent and flourishing group of business people who were making a lot of money. Among these were college students. However, since some of their activities were unclear to me, I decided not to be involved with this group.

As I time went by, I continued to increase the network of people I knew and would affiliate with. I met new people from all over the world and here in the U.S. as well. I would socialize and go out to different spots in hopes of meeting that girl I would want to start my family with, but my over analytical side would dominate my interactions. Hoping that I could meet her on the dance floor, I added more step to my groove on the dance floor except now I would add gyrations to my hips and I would wear my brown kango to add flavor to my swag. I wooed many ladies and developed a reputation as a player, but I was educated too and it seemed I was unable to find an intellectual or even spiritual connection at the same time.

To diversify my game, I would show off my physical abilities on the basketball floor and soccer field, which games I excelled. My health and appearance at this time in June of 1997 was even better than when I began taking things seriously in the spring of 1996, albeit I had a random nagging feeling but I did not let it slow me down. Although I looked superb and happy, there still was a void in me, which (I now understand) was not with me alone but with everyone who went on our trip to Ghana. It was I think the separation from our daily adventures and communion we had with one another.

Like many others, music and friends were my consolation, but it would all remind me of my trip and that girl I met in Ghana. I remember meeting another black girl in her room named Lucy, who was listening to this artist named Erykah Badu and the song was called 'Next Lifetime', which reminded me more of that Ghanaian girl and I was thinking that our next encounter would be as butterflies or something. Lucy was an interesting girl, but my mind was still in Ghana. Around this time and as part of my connection with the ASA, I also met George, an Eritrean guy, and in utter surprise for both of us, we realized that we met at Koko Beta Beach in Ghana. He introduced me to his sister Serena. First of all, I must say that Eritreans are some very cool people and meeting and talking to him about Ghana was therapeutic for me. Also, Julie was another girl that I liked a lot. We had our private moments, created pet names for each other as I called her my 'Butterfly' and she called me 'Nehemiah the tiger', because my body was so chiseled and superb. Even though she was gorgeous too, I felt she put on a front that she was a tough fighter, which I did not like. Furthermore, she was a Ghanaian girl who I got close with. This click of friends were my ongoing support group as now both Ghana and Uganda were part of my history, but Ghana more recently. I cherished these friends and it made me feel good that I had a big part of me in both countries. Sweet memories were accrued with these guys as we would go to movies, out to restaurants and dancing, which is where I got to showcase my dance steps.

In the summer of 1997, I bought my red Mazda 626 using some of the funds I still had from my law suit settlement. This vehicle coupled with my physical appearance gave me the complete package and I would shine on the dance floor, basketball court, soccer field and I had a good social life too.

In addition to these accomplishments, my aspirations to continue my education were heavy on my mind as well. I wanted to have a business of some sort and have a graduate degree as well that would not bury me in debt. As I would ponder this strategy, my mom told me that in January of 1998 she was planning a trip to Uganda and I knew this was my calling especially since I already had most of my immunizations from my trip to Ghana that were necessary for Uganda. I was excited to see my country of birth and meet many of my aunties, uncles and cousins that I only knew via the telephone.

I was excited and ready for what was in front of me as my physical workouts intensified as well as my dancing with my kango as an expression of my alter-ego of a smooth, big money player. With all this going on, I began to realize that I needed to pursue a post graduate degree where I would make a lot of money.

An MBA would be my choice and a local state university would be my school of choice as it was in my back yard. My only obstacle, which was my nemesis was the standardized testing to gain my admission, the GMAT. Much like the ACT for college admission and more recently the LSAT, which I battled with significantly to get into Law School, the GMAT soon became my endless battle.

It did not take long however for a local state university to make a decision to admit me. I believe this was so because of my life experience I had accumulated up to this point in addition to my ability to communicate in writing. Indeed there was some buzzing in the Ugandan community and with my friends because those letters 'M.B.A' carried a lot of weight, but I personally had no clear idea what I would do with this degree. Notwithstanding this fact, I would start my schooling in the spring, and to prepare myself I would read the "Wall Street Journal" and read articles by Warren Buffett as I took to heart his words that 'you should buy when no one else is and sell when everyone else is buying'. These words did not mean much to me at the time, but my trip to Uganda was at hand and we were set to depart for our trip.

My friends were still impressed that I just was in Ghana and I was on en route to Uganda with our first stop in Brussels, Belgium. By this time I had started communicating with my girl friend in Ghana at least twice a week. I told her I was going back to Africa, specifically Uganda.

It was at this time that I heard back from Dave the realtor who let me know that there was an opportunity to purchase a property and that he had a buddy who could help me with the financing. I did not know anything about this type of business except what I was exposed to through from his own experiences. Nonetheless, I was a willing participant and he called me into his office where we spoke of a rental property on the southeast side of town that had a lot of potential. We proceeded to look at it and I was impressed with his salesmanship and next thing I knew is that we were soon writing a purchase agreement and looking at a closing table.

My mind nonetheless was on Uganda and my expectations were somewhat set from my trip to Ghana. The feeling that came over me when we arrived in Brussels, Belgium was amazing as I realized how diverse this world is since at the airport one could choose to use English, French, German or Dutch. But that did not compare to Entebbe international airport in Uganda where I was greeted by my family members I had never met before. I was overjoyed to meet some of my cousins – Geraldine Nzinga, Emmanuel Mulungi, Dyna Namatende, Flora Kasuswa, Fida Namususwa, and Joshua Magezi.

This was therapeutic to my soul as I truly felt my present getting connected to my past. Additionally, it put things in perspective as my grannies did not speak any English and my mom and family members were my interpreters as I realized my comprehension of Lusoga was limited. One example is when we went to a rural area such as Lulyambuzi (my mom's birth place),and attended a church service where I was totally at a loss because it was conducted in Lusoga a language I was not conversant with. However, when we visited Buwaiswa (my father's birth place) we came across English speakers such as Uncle John (my dad's older brother). My experience meeting him was exciting for both my sister and I because he spoke English in the countryside where no one was speaking English and he looked like my dad.

Indeed, I love my country and my people. I loved the daily greetings at our home in Jinja as neighbors would walk by. I realized how cordial and polite we really are as a people when a simple 'hello, how are you?' or in Lusoga 'mulimutya eyo' would turn into a twenty minutes greeting and visiting people on a daily basis for extended periods of time as if things have changed ten thousand fold from the day before. What made this experience perhaps hysterical is when my brother Joshua Magezi disappeared and joined a local campaign effort that was traveling from house to house in Jinja. He knew nobody in that campaign or what they were campaigning about. Mom had a perplexed look on her face when she was doing a roll call of her children and realized that Joshua was not there, but later came home after 9-10 hours.

We traveled to Kampala (the capital of Uganda) where I met Abel (father of one of my friends back in the states) from Eritrea. At this time, I presented him gifts from his children and passed regards from them, as well. He was working for the United Nations at that time and even though I was in my country of birth, he brought another side to my Eritrean experience. When in Kampala we went to the marketplaces and one thing I noticed was that people would speak to me in Luganda (one of Uganda's languages) in Kampala or Lusoga (the language spoken in Jinja). This at first made me uncomfortable since English was not widely used in Uganda. This was a major contrast with Ghana which because of its long contacts with the West, English is used even by ordinary people. Another major observation I had was that the driving was on the right side and people drove recklessly without using seatbelts.

Perhaps a big change in Uganda versus my trip to Ghana was the fact that I was not a tourist, but I was a commoner with my family in Jinja at Madhvani road. I learned a lot about myself and my personality based on how we would interact with people both as a family and collectively which was my desire to always greet people and stay friendly at all costs.

My sister Dyna Namatende won the immigration lottery to come to the USA and we traveled to Nairobi, Kenya to finalize this process. We took a bus and we realized how bad the main highway from Kampala to Nairobi was. I thought the bus had broken down or fallen apart as we drove on steep meandering roads. Due to the poor roads, the trip was longer than would be the case in the USA.

We stopped at the border between Uganda and Kenya and we were met with an unforeseen situation, which in hindsight, was handled very interestingly. Specifically, my sister Monica and I, who are natural born Ugandans, were told to pay a $60 fee individually for reasons the security agent with a rifle said had to do with the fact that our passports were American and not Ugandan or Kenyan. I did not know the legitimacy of this request but since I was not armed, I did not hesitate to give the man $60; but Monica, on the other hand, did not acquiesce to his request immediately, but she insisted that she was a Ugandan citizen and the man had no right to ask for the $60. Indeed, she had a point, Monica is well educated, but I am not sure that the man understood her or even knew why she would make a big deal about it especially with the bus revving its engine ready to leave with or without us and leave us in the middle of nowhere at the border of Uganda and Kenya. Monica eventually paid the required amount and demanded to get a receipt. To the surprise of everyone, the boarder guard became agitated and raised a puzzling question – "Why are you asking for a receipt? Do you think I am a thief?" Today we still joke about this incident because of how close we were to interrupting our plans of getting Dyna's visa in Nairobi.

Finally, we arrived at Nairobi! This city was incredible in that it was metropolis with the driving and steering done on the right side but there were warnings in English on the buses that jewelry and valuables should be out of sight with thieves snatching and stealing them regardless of where they were located on the body and beggars were eyeing down tourists looking to hustle as much money as possible. This was a tourist city and so the first thing we did was go to the exchange bureau. I think in hindsight that there were professional beggars working 9-5 that knew we had entered the exchange because the beggars intensified when we showed the tellers U.S. dollars and travelers' checks we were exchanging. Interestingly furthermore, my sister and I were followed for almost a mile as we were walking downtown by a woman who had an object under a blanket saying it was her baby who had not eaten in days, but we observed that there was no baby with her, but only a ball. I love to give, but I detected that this woman was a true beggar and so we ignored her until she gave up. With this woman out of the way, we started enjoying the Nairobi surroundings. Nairobi had a very dynamic marketplaces where many items were sold and interestingly things were for sale in dollars and not shillings, the local currency. One of the unusual thing was that if you wanted a good bargain, then you would pay in dollars instead of the local Kenya Shillings.

All in all, I enjoyed visiting Nairobi. I wish we went to Mombasa and seen more of Kenya, but it was time to head back to Uganda. On our way back, we were met by the same shady gatekeeper, who was fully armed and ready to check passports and collect the dues; we paid him and got on the bus with no discussion. This trip to Nairobi finalized our Kenyan experience and Dyna was legally ready to come to the states. Indeed, I do not know what other things mom, dad and Dyna had to do to get ready but we had time left in Uganda and I wanted to see the nightlife. This desire had me thinking about the girl from Ghana and I started to wonder if I would meet a special girl in Uganda. To date, I am not exactly sure why I wanted a bride from Africa when I was raised in the states and there were plenty to choose from there, but I did speak, perhaps prophetically to myself when I was a child that I would someday marry an African girl.

Emmanuel Mulungi was not a clubber and mom was not ready to let us explore the night life in Kampala, understandably. Instead we experienced everyday life in Jinja, which included going to the local marketplace for supplies where one event that stands out to me is when a woman was sleeping on her job when she was supposed to sell us items and commodities. Instead she asked us in Lusoga where we were from and what language we spoke as my sister and I did not live there or were commoners. This was funny, nonetheless, as Nairobi was more of a non-stop hustle in contrast to what transpired at this point. Perhaps that was because Jinja was a smaller town where everyone knew almost everyone else. I purchased some nice memorabilia in Nairobi, but I bought whatever I could in Jinja since my time in Uganda was running out and besides Jinja is my home and I wanted memorabilia I would show to my children in the future.

After visiting everyone we could in the time allotted, we began our departure back to the states. This departure was emotional and all I knew to do was not say goodbye, but 'until we meet again.' The flight was smooth and this time after arriving back home, I took time off of work. It did not take long to recover and going back to my 9-5 and reflecting on what this trip meant to me was precious. I also got back into my work out routine immediately after my rest and I began to notice that my life as I perceived it in took on a whole new meaning than it did before. I was still receiving letters from my adopted friends in Ghana and I would still call the girl in Ghana as I had her number and my relationship with my Student Association friends tightened, as well. I never knew the depths of my actions at this time with what I was going through. I knew that I needed to continue my education as I was already admitted to the graduate school in business.

CHAPTER 3

Mapping My Future: Pursuing a Graduate Degree; Adventures in Real Estate Business; Getting a Reliable Job; Issues on the Social Front

Realizing that the pursuit of such a degree would widen my opportunities such as getting a reliable job and making more travels to Africa, I decided to start on my graduate degree in Spring. Even though I read a lot of books and studied a lot in college, I really did not know what business school specifically entailed.

Nonetheless, things were definitely changing in my life and beginning to take form on the academic, business and social front, but I wanted a steady girlfriend that I could call my own and she could do the same. I was still talking to Joan and other girls on the home front and I liked Joan a lot, but there was always a schism in our relationship that I felt inhibited me from making the move I wanted to. Again, I really liked her and i thought she was attractive and funny but I over analyzed everything in our situation that was not practical, in hindsight. Nonetheless, Joan and her baby Agartha became a big part of my daily life. I think, in hindsight, that part of what was slowing us down was the fact that her baby was just born and Aida and her (ex) boyfriend were not together. Notwithstanding this fact, Joan was a good mom, her baby was happy and we grew closer and closer by the day.

Julie was another girl that I liked a lot. She was a Ghanaian girl who attended one of the universities in the cities who I also got close with. She was friends with the son of the man who picked me up in Accra that I was now friends with along with the aforementioned Ugandan girl from a successful family. This click of friends and the Student Association were my ongoing support group as now both Ghana and Uganda trips were part of my recent history. I cherished these friends and it made me feel good that I had a big part of my life in both countries. Good times and nice memories were accrued with all these people, as we would go to movies, out to restaurants and dancing, which is where I got to showcase my dance step. We were all in school, as I was en route to complete my masters since I had started with some classes.

Coupled with these friends, I would also travel to one of the state colleges and spend time with another girl named Katirine from Kenya. She represented to me a side of Kenya that I was not very familiar with. She was a college student at one of the state colleges and she was determined as I was. Beside the physical attraction we really had nothing in common. Nonetheless, we would go out to dinner, movies and cuddle but we left it at that. At this time, I still kept in touch with that girl from Ghana on an occasional basis to keep in contact with part of that experience.

In the interim, I was taking more classes towards my degree and I was building more relationships on the social front with school and all. I was a one-man machine in everything I did. My network of friends included friends from every corner of the world. I would occasionally go out on dates with an Asian girl from Laos, who I met at a social function at a home town state university. However, as it turned out, there were no commonalities, aside from physical attraction. I knew that my appearance was stunning; I had a good personality; I was educated, and I was an incredible dancer, but why could I not find that perfect fit? This was my quest and soon became my dilemma. Interestingly at this time, my older brother asked me to become the best man in his wedding to Eseza, which I accepted, and that gave me a better insight into the beauty of the married world.

At this time, my conversations with the girl from my trip to Ghana would continue and I would tell her how I could bring her to the U.S. on a fiancé visa. I began to advise her how to conduct herself before the US consulate at the embassy and I began to have meaningful conversations with her, as much as I could. We started to say 'I love you' as we spoke on the phone and exchanged love letters

The next hurdle was telling mom and dad what my plan was. I told them how I had fallen in 'love with a girl from Ghana and I wanted to bring her to the USA. They were very skeptical of my idea and tried to emphasize that I should slow down because I did not know her well enough. But I did not take their advice and I continued on with my plan.

On the home front from a business perspective, I pressed on as I continued to look for my next hustle. I met people who were from different areas of the world, but I would mesh well with West Africans best because of my recent trip to Ghana, even though I am Ugandan by birth. I remembered the time I spent going to historical places and dancing till the sun came up. It would leave me with a void that my time there was so brief and I had no one to share those memories with. Again, the Student Association brought me comfort. The guy who led the trip from our school seemed to know the need to provide comfort and support to those of us who went as he would always refer to our trip in the present tense which made it seem like it was on going. I would later find out that there were others from the trip that needed the same type of support.

I graduated from college in 96', I went to Ghana in 97' and then Uganda in '98 and '99 had something else in store as I was soon to close on my first home and met up with my girlfriend from Ghana. Additionally, in December of '98, I had made several new friends (one of whom was George from Eritrea that I had met at Koko Beta beach in Ghana '97) and they were all looking for my next move which again was buying my first home and I needed a girl I could call my own. George was dating a Ghanaian girl and I told him I wanted to marry a girl from

Ghana, but he advised me to the contrary. Interestingly, the girl he was seeing was also suspect, to me, as she looked to be questionable in her general demeanor. She was attending my almamater and I could also see that she was determined and independent, too.

It was at this time, in January of 1999 that I found myself at a closing table ready to buy my first house. The closing was not smooth, but I would later find out that many of them never go as planned, but we got it done. I was a homeowner and a landlord, which I knew nothing about! Just as Dave guided me into buying the home, I also wanted guidance in being a landlord. He had his own business with real estate and rental homes and so not only did I listen to him but I watched his actions as he would resolve and disseminate issues. My biggest issue at the time was what to do after receiving $1500 after closing, with 60 days before my first payment, with $2200 in rent checks on deck for February. I told no one but my parents and friends what I had done and I was careful not to sound like I was boasting, but I listened attentively to what people were saying about rental management, in general since I was expecting multiple calls from tenants looking to get out of either paying rent or just give me a headache. Interestingly, Dave contacted me again (within weeks of purchasing this home) to sell it, as he had a buyer and told me I could make $10,000.

At this time, I began to intensify the frequency of calling my girlfriend in Ghana. We began to call each other chocolate and I even sent her a cassette single from Blackstreet entitled 'Don't leave me girl' as we both yearned about wanting to meet again. She presented a convincing argument of how everyone had abandoned her leaving her to take care of herself. I felt sorry for her, not even knowing the other side of the story! I took on her burden as if it was mine and started calling her more frequently. I was not financially where I wanted to be, but I would send her money and pictures of me, my family and my Mazda 626 as much as my time and resources afforded. She also sent me pictures of herself and wrote me letters, which showed her lack of formal education.

In the interim, I was getting adjusted to being a landlord and coming to terms with the fact that it was my house. I would drive by the home frequently, analyze things and try to apply the business theories I was learning in management classes, and that made me feel more like the business man I was going to school for. Collecting rents was effortless as my tenants were low maintenance and I would go to my PO Box, pick up rents and deposit them into my account. My mom did counsel me to separate my personal money from my business account. Without a mortgage payment, I added another $1400 into my account, but I knew I had to pay for my tuition, property taxes and maintenance plus send some money to my girlfriend in Ghana and on top of all this, payment for two months would start so would the hustling.

My first real challenge as a landlord was when I received a 60 day notice from one of my tenants in my new house. At first I took it personal, but I realized that this was a part of the business I had taken as my own, and I also was looking for a place to live since I was bringing my girlfriend whom I now call 'Baby' to the states from Africa. Again, this whole property management thing (and importing an unknown girl to be my wife, which I prophesied over myself as a young boy) was unchartered territory with me and my family's plight, but I had to make it work!

In the meanwhile, I created flyers and told all my friends at the university that I had a vacancy coming up, but, I remembered the advice I was given from Dave (who sold me the house). He advised me not to rent to friends, to advertise in the local papers and keep all the receipts related to whatever transaction I carried out.

It was at this time, moreover, that I found just how in high demand these properties were. This home was close enough to the local universities and the Technical College where one ad caused over 400 phone calls and showings with a $20 nonrefundable application fee per showing from me. This surge in cash flow allowed me to pay for my property taxes, get a jump start on my mortgage, send money to my girlfriend in Ghana, and still have some cash flow for myself on the domestic front. I also would put in extra hours at work in order to procure additional funds for my other projects. I felt a sense of accomplishment and managed to bring my girlfriend to the USA.

Soon after her arrival, I realized how much I did not know about this girl from Africa. I had to identify myself at the airport in order for her to recognize me! Once the (re) introduction ended I had to give a crash course into Minnesota weather in March and I tried to communicate to her that I did not have health insurance for her, as well. Given her limited English, I am not sure she understood much of what I was explaining. Fortunately, I had friends from Ghana who explained many things in her "native" language.

Notwithstanding this drama, I felt good about what was in front of me. I was taking more classes towards my master's degree and I had to travel out of town on a business trip. Then next obligation I had was introducing my girlfriend to my parents and the rest of my family. Despite the reservations, family members welcomed her. My mother accepted her as her own child and taught her some lifelong human skills that somebody who does not know you well would not bother to teach you. One of these skills was teaching her how to drive a car. In spite of the love my family showed her, she constantly complained how everybody hated her. I comforted her as much as I could.

Since I brought her to the states on a Fiancé visa, I only had three months to wed her. Thus although I did not know her well enough, I was under pressure to make a decision to wed her. In the short time I spent with her, I did not really love her like I wanted to love a woman. I could only remember the epiphany I had when I first met her, but I did not see all the drama with it. Nonetheless I come from a family that has helped many people both in the states and in Africa. I also could see that she needed my help as not marrying her, but sending her away, could be more problematic for her given she had no practical or marketable skills. Now that I brought her here, I figured she needed to know the real life (dog eat dog world) in the states as opposed to the artificial world portrayed on the TV. I therefore decided that since I have come this far with the process, I needed to see it through, at least until she got her papers.

A crash course into Minnesota living was not easy with 'Baby' because not only did I realize that much of what I was saying to her was not understood by her. Also I realized that she did not have the education or practical skills that would allow her to work most jobs. Additionally, she slept until 3pm in the afternoon. She also liked to get into daily heated arguments over irrelevant issues. I could not see myself growing old with this girl, either. Since I was not comfortable with all this, I needed to tell her that we should separate. But she would always tell me, via Email, that once her situation was settled with her 'peppars' or papers, she would move on.

Nonetheless, our (my) life at that point consisted of me going to my $8 an hour job with no benefits and working 50+ hours a week, while she would lie around and sleep till I got home. Also, her hygiene was very poor as she would not brush her teeth, take a shower, fold her clothes, do laundry or even cook or clean. All she would tell me that nobody taught her these things. But my sympathy turned simply to disgust as no matter what I said to correct the behavior she was content living in that chaos. To complicate things, she wanted to start having children right away. I unsuccessfully failed to convince her that starting a family involves careful planning from the would be parents. Thus, I refused and discouraged her from having children at this time and went to planned parenting because I also do not believe in abortion.

She would speak with people on the telephone non-stop mostly in African languages which at first I did not mind. However, some of the people she spoke to that I understood were giving her sketchy advice such as requesting that I pay a dowry for her and extort money from me, even though I did not have anything to give. Notwithstanding this fact, I could see by the looks she would give me and her subsequent actions that she wanted me out of the picture of her life. Sensing this, I suggested that since we were not meant to be married, it would be beneficial to separate. The moment I raised this, the apparent schizophrenic aspect of her personality erupted. She started crying saying that our relationship was meant forever and that if I did not bring her to the USA she would have died on the streets in Accra. She then would say if we got separated or she died and I pursued another girl, she would come back from the dead and haunt anybody I would date or marry! To lessen this stress, I would exercise or play basketball or soccer but the nagging feeling in my body slowed me down.

As things financially were fickle for me, I continued to speak with Dave for more opportunities to acquire rental properties and being a good salesman, he indicated that there was an opportunity to purchase another rental property. I immediately capitalized on this opportunity and before I knew it, I owned my second home.

I received some more cash flow which I needed to support my family. The only caveat I had with this deal was that property taxes were due in two months and there was the problem of getting rid of the tenants who were living in the newest house. The headache to get these people out was tremendous, but so was the learning experience.

On the home front, I knew I needed to get 'Baby' health insurance and employment. I believed first that it was my duty to teach her how to drive so she could find a job or get herself into an opportunity where she would get paid. I decided to start with the basics one July evening. I took her out to a parking lot one afternoon with no people around. There were only a few unoccupied cars (thank God!). What transpired after words is to this day a miracle because there were no fatalities between 'Baby' or I. I instructed 'Baby' as to how to go slowly and make sure she was buckled, but as soon as she got behind the wheel, she punched it. The empty car in front of us is the only reason we slowed down or stopped as the damage was substantial both physically and collaterally to my vehicle and to my body. I could not function or think properly after the accident as my arm was profusely bleeding and I was not sure who would pay the medical bills. Fortunately, I remembered later that my car insurance will pay for my injuries. I still waited eight hours before checking into the hospital.

You live once, but in an instant not only was my 626 gone in a total loss accident, but my physicality was adversely affected because of my delay to treat my arm. Also, I was diagnosed with vertigo as I was dealing with nonstop imbalance, nausea and occasional muscle tightening, and there was something else bothering me that was not diagnosed. Nonetheless, this was another anomaly that was added into my book of ailments. Basically, I once had the appearance of a Roman gladiator, but now I looked like a lost and vulnerable child.

Since I now did not have a car, I borrowed one from my parents. This tremendously helped me to continue handling my daily activities. At about this time I developed vertigo which the doctor could not immediately treat. Through this all, 'Baby' did not understand the magnitude of what just transpired or could have happened if that empty car was not there to stop us or if someone was in the vicinity. She, too, thought that riding in the old car my parents loaned me was beneath her dignity. Because of her nonchalant behavior, I became suspicious as to her intentions with staying in my life. I also could not come to terms as to how insensitive and pretentious she is.

Life went on, nonetheless, and the good thing that came from this incident is that I received a $2000 dollar check from the insurance company because I had equity in my vehicle. This check allowed me to pay my property taxes on my rental properties and left me some extra money for a down payment on another car (1995 Chrysler Sebring) which I purchased from a local car dealership in the area.

On the home front, I was dealing with difficult tenants at my new home who I had no choice but to evict. I had sleepless nights because I had never experienced having to remove bad tenants and facing the challenges of paying the rental mortgage from my personal funds. Due to the complexity of Minnesota laws, the wait for the eviction notice was endless. What further complicated my situation was that the tenants were low-class arrogant ones who seriously did not believe that a black person could evict them from the house. But when the judge issued the writ of the eviction was relatively simple as the sheriff facilitated the process. All in all, this whole process was costly and burdensome, but I received phone calls from perspective tenants who were friends of some other tenants I had had and the 'cash flow' continued. Additionally, 'Baby' got a part-time job at a local company in town which was the largest employer at that time.

To lessen some of the stress I had experienced, we went to Las Vegas for a vacation. Although the trip was refreshing, I discovered a new dimension of 'Baby' personality, namely her insecurity and being pretentiousness. The range of emotions when we played slot machines and won some money was incredible, but that was immediately followed by rage when an unknown cocktail waitress would walk by me and ask me for a drink in a flirtatious manner. These events in Vegas spoke volumes to me, coupled with her disconnected behavior when I was struggling to get my nonpaying tenants out of my rental house and tried to communicate with her about my nagging body. I remember how she acted disinterested in helping me rebound emotionally from the total loss of my Mazda 626 or my physical ailments.

After the Vegas trip in 1999, I felt rejuvenated and was ready to get back to the grind. Work was steady, my houses were occupied with paying tenants and 'Baby' was settled and working maybe 10-15 hours a week. But she was even more dependent on me, nonetheless. Specifically, I would drive everywhere, take her out to eat on a weekly basis, pick her up from work and she became higher maintenance, while she would fight and argue with me over irrelevant things. The friends she would make were also suspect to me one of whom was an African-American called Anita. I believe this woman was indoctrinating her with a victimized woman's state of mind (as she may have legitimately been in an abusive relationship). It was about this time when she started swearing and cursing at me with the objective of provoking me. The toxic relationship continued on several fronts: she would stay up until 3a.m watching Nigerian movies; talking loudly with someone on the phone; and then coming to bed when I was asleep and deliberately made noises to wake me up knowing I had to wake at 6am.

Some nights around 3am when I was in a deep sleep, I would feel like I was suffocating in my dream, and several times I could feel my spirit leave my body. In some instances, she would call the police alleging that I had abused her. I was locked up but was let go once they realized that I was an innocent law-abiding citizen. At the same time she made false accusations about me and she would out of the blue indicate how much she loved me, narrate stories about her family in Ghana and how we would have a bright future together. These positive statements about me notwithstanding, it became clear every day that probably this was an unbalanced person who should be left alone.

Rather than officially end this toxic social relationship, I worked on the false assumption that if I amassed more wealth, it would probably be helpful in making us work together. Consequently, I contacted my real estate person Dave and indicated to him that I wanted to purchase another property. I needed some money to get this condo and my sister

Olivia, even though she did not have much, she lent me some funds. Subsequently, in March of 2000, I put in an offer to purchase a nice condo in downtown. I closed on it in April of 2000 and now I owned three homes at once.

Acquiring a third home enabled me to have funds for use on several projects: I paid off my student loans; paid cash for tuition for my graduate degree; had funds left over for family use; and developed a close relationship with a CPA who guided me into the complex rules and regulations relating to business in general and property management in particular. Despite my shaky social relationship, I also opened up communication with more Africans in general and Ghanaians in particular. The relationship I made with Africans was therapeutic for me in that it further helped me strengthen my identity and kept the African experience I acquired fresh in my head. I for example, was forced to remember the children I met in Ghana and helped them for a while after I returned to the USA. Perhaps even more touching than all this was that my interaction with the Africans in the USA brought fresh memory about relatives I met in Uganda.

However, I realized that soon after the purchase of my third property, I needed to sell or refinance the mortgages on my rental properties since they were each on sub-prime balloon mortgages, set to adjust in January of 2001. I was barely cash flowing on these houses, but since my tenants would move out and make lease violations, I would capitalize on these mistakes and make money. Additionally, I was making a lot of cash in bonuses and commissions from my job, but the job itself was volatile. But I still needed to make a move. I knew Rob could have sold these three homes in no time at all and I would have made $120k to $150k between them; but that would end this landlord experience for me. Even though my full-time job was relatively volatile, I also enjoyed collecting rents, paying the mortgages and realizing a cash flow. Also to sell my rental properties would bring a fairly hefty capital gains penalty, which scared me since I knew nothing about.

I was paying my bills but I was not comfortable with the loan officer Dave was working with and so I looked into other options. The real estate and banking industry was also warming up and I received non-stop mailings from different mortgage brokers, many of whom looked shady and different real estate companies to buy/sell homes (some of whom I knew personally). One mailing I received was from a bank whose loan officer had several years of experience originating loans. Realizing that "Baby" may not be in agreement about my refinancing with this loan officer because she was an attractive woman, I met the loan officer privately and explained situation. Once she told me that she could get it done, I did not hesitate to advertise the fact that she is a good loans officer working for a good bank. After everything was in place, both 'Baby' and I signed the refinancing application forms.

I did not realize it at the time, but this transaction would change the dynamic of both my real estate ventures and relationship with 'Baby', who I still did not want to be my wife. I met Kevin, the appraiser, who appraised the homes for over $30000 than what I bought them for. He spoke adversely about Rob, nonetheless; but I still had respect for Rob's hustle because if he did not sell me the homes, I would not be in this business to begin with. Nonetheless, once the loan officer finished processing the transaction I received a two month break from mortgage payments, with tenants paying me totaling $5200 for two months. She showed me that the payments on each house would also go down by $500 with taxes and insurance escrowed, totaling $1000 a month additional cash flow. All in all, I would put over $5000 in my pocket, with no worries about a tax payment or even insurance payment and over $80000 in equity, per my appraisals.

I had the cash flow to pay for my tuition, I finished paying off the loans I had from college, paid down my car loan substantially, and this success would bring responsibility. One such responsibility was the realization that I needed to assist my parents who sponsored my relatives to come study in the USA. In addition to sponsoring regular students, they also had taken on a very expensive project of adapting two of my young cousins (Fida and Joshua). As I learned from my parents, immigrant visas are both complex in processing and are very expensive. I am grateful that although my contribution to help my relatives come to the USA was modest, I felt blessed that I was of some assistance.

However, while I made modest progress on the business front, my social life was in a mess. I did not stop to evaluate how much of a roller-coaster 'Baby' was to me, in my personal life. I was actually lonely even though she was here with me. I did not want her to mother my children and I did not know if this was my destiny, or punishment for something I did, or just a circumstance in my life that would pass. I needed God in my life for answers because she was frequently bringing me down with her non-stop argumentative level. Beside an occasional service at the local church that made me feel good, I felt void when I had questions about what was preached or general questions about the text that was read from the bible. I asked a lot of questions as my liberal arts education had groomed my thinking as such. I realized that God gave me the ability to bring her here, take care of her and continue on with a destiny that I was striving for and this was not by accident. I truly believed He would conclude it as He saw fit. But this was a needed peace, nonetheless, and 'Baby', like all my other endeavors would follow me to church because, I think, she thought I had a girlfriend there as she would accuse me of having an affair to substantiate my hunch. Secondly I think she would attend with me because she wanted to know what was being said.

Immediately she forgot about the grace that was preached and she would go back to her argumentative non-sense. I could see what kind of peace it was giving my peers and I thought maybe it could happen between her and I, but the 'writing on the wall' would speak to the contrary as vulgarities would dominate her speech to me. At the end of the day, moreover, she was not going anywhere but insisted on fighting with me and on waiting to see what would happen, and subsequently, people began to see us as a couple because we were not separating.

I eventually picked up some divorce papers from the county, but 'Baby' would locate them, read them through and then destroy them and leave them out as if to insinuate that it would take more than a document to separate us. I had no time to invest my energy into social issues since I had many things working in my favor (schooling, working and doing business on the side).

I must also comment that even though there were many difficult times, not all times were bad. As I previously noted, I took her to Las Vegas where we enjoyed some good times, even though things were difficult for me with my rental properties at that time on the home front and tenants (and we still had a turbulent episodes of fighting over nothing while we were there). We also began to eat out at some fairly nice restaurants two to three times a week, such as Red Lobster and Olive Garden. This became so regular that people working at these restaurants probably were not sure if had won thousands of dollars in gift certificates. Also, I did not realize at that time that the funds I was spending on eating out reinforced her bad habits of poor hygiene at the house in the kitchen and disregard for etiquette in the fridge or even frugality with money, for that matter.

As 2000 was coming to an end, I realized that many of my peers were moving ahead with their careers. At this time, I was disconnected from what was happening although I was set to graduate in the spring. Thus, I knew I needed to have a big picture in my life since my home town was changing and I did not want to make this place my permanent home. Additionally, as I was working towards my MBA, I was also completing my Associates Degree in computer science at a local Technical College. I interviewed with a few companies but I was unsuccessful. Therefore, my New Years of 2001 presented a new commitment for me which was to increase my computer programming and general programming skills plus general knowledge and the ability to master the interview.

Thus, I purchased a book from Barnes and Noble on mastering the interview. This book gave mock interview questions and what would be asked and how the interviewee should answer. I would practice these every day and 'Baby' did not know what was going on with my practicing and she would not ask either. I would leave the book in the same spot so she could read it if she wanted and I know she did.

Nonetheless she would laugh at me as I would practice for the interview and the senseless fighting would continue between us with her swearing as she would tell me how much she wanted to get to the cities. My confidence, nonetheless, increased substantially for the big interview although I did not know when that would be. I also learned at this time that many of the people interviewing for technical jobs like I was shooting for did not know very much as far as the technical know how with programming because the education being provided at the university, in my opinion, was more theory oriented than practical.

It was March of 2001 when there was a big job fair at a local state university. I was ready for the interview since my appearance was stunning and my personality and smile were on point. This fair was more of a screening before the big interview, but I knew that making a good first impression with the gate keeper was vitally important.

My impressive stature and competitive instinct paid off at this job fair as I was relentless in my pursuit to better myself and I interviewed with three companies, but there were two of which I really liked. I brought my 'A' game of first impression to all three interviews and the gatekeepers invited me in for the interview where I could show them who I was. This gave them a chance to learn about me I also learned about their companies.

Fortunately, one of these companies offered me a job. My emotions took over me when they sent me the offer because I was working diligently for this chance to move ahead with my career. I told my mom and dad about the offer as I was emotional, but I made the mistake of telling 'Baby' with my offer letter in my hand, conversely, because she thought the endless money tree had just added more funds for her. Not understanding how the USA system works when it comes to looking for employment, I think she thought I was doing something criminal. I say that without being cynical because we were not getting along. She was not ready to get out of my life and she continued to curse me out as an avenue for her general disdain for how wrong she feels she was done in her life. Additionally, many of her phone calls were often screaming to people in some sort of English and sometimes easily comprehendible speech that she has been victimized. But she liked this ride she was on with me and I think the victim rhetoric just gave her an impression as to how things generally work in this society to protect the disadvantaged in a relationship. Nonetheless, as a side note, the third company also gave me an offer, but they were in bill collections which I declined because I did not want to stay in that line of work.

The starting date was June 1, 2001 and so this gave me time to prepare for my new assignment. One decision I had to make was what to do with my rental properties. I was not ready to part with them since they provided me with cash and yet retaining them involved the continued dealings with recalcitrant (refusing to pay rent or trashing the property) tenants. I also was faced with the challenge of either selling my personal home in order to be closer to my place of wok or commute a distance of close to 150 miles every day. These challenges notwithstanding, I felt good about my achievements: I successfully completed my MBA and thereby demonstrating the value my family and I attached to education; I was offered a reliable job; and I was doing modestly well in the real estate business. In recognition of all this, my parents gave me a graduation party.

With the party festivities over, it was time to start my job at an insurance company. I contacted my real estate advisor so that he could put my condo on the market. The first weak my condo was listed, there were roughly 20 showings, but no offers. As I later found out, part of the problem was that the condo was filthy due to my inability to be at two places at the same time – at home cleaning the house and at work which was 150 miles round trip. 'Baby" neither understood what was going on nor did she really care about what I was trying to do. Consequently, the first two months of my work were highlighted by stress resulting from the long commute I had to make every day, toxic social conditions in the house, and inability to sell the condo, despite the hot real estate market that was prevalent at the time. As expected, my job performance was compromised. The sad thing about all this was that there were no facilities at work to help new employees who faced challenges like I was confronted with.

By the grace of God, I finally sold my condo in my home town and I had to move to the "Twin Cities" which was closer to my work place. Leaving my home town meant that I had to find a way I would efficiently manage my property from a distance of 75 miles. Given the little experience I had about this, I signed an agreement with a Property Management Company. Fortunately, the company I signed the agreement with had an employee whom I had attended the same high school with. This initially helped me greatly because aside from collecting rent, this company also assisted me in advertising vacancies whenever they became open and stayed honest in their financial dealings with me.

My next move was to find a place where to stay in the "Twin Cities". Using the decent funds I made selling my condo, I purchased a condo within the vicinity of my work place. The company initially treated me well, particularly with work related matters. For example, before I could settle down, the company sent me to San Francisco on an employee only trip. This one-week conference was refreshing on two fronts – I learned a lot about my company in general and my job in particular and secondly in spite of the non-stop phone calls I got from "Baby", I was relieved to be away from the prevailing toxic social environment in my home.

Soon after my trip, I got a call from "Baby" at work and she told me she was pregnant. I thought this was good news which would bring us closer in our relationship. This good news was later followed by the exciting offer the company gave me to go to Chicago for another conference. Since spouses were allowed to go to this conference, "Baby" accompanied me. In the evenings we took a subway to different locations and went sight-seeing.

While in training the next morning on September 11, 2001 right outside the Sears Tower, we witnessed on television the most catastrophic event in American history when two planes high jacked by terrorists flew into the World Trade Tower in Manhattan, New York killing thousands of people. Our conference thereafter was cut short and we drove home in a state of anxiety, bewilderment, fear, and just total confusion. It also demonstrated to me how vulnerable we are as human beings!!

My enjoyable early work conditions at my new job were compromised by the poor health experience I encountered. It all started with a nagging feeling in my stomach which always occurred soon after eating lunch at the company cafeteria. The discomfort in the stomach was followed by vomiting which temporarily made me a hostage to the bathroom. What is sad and depressing was that none of my co-workers tried to find out what exactly was happening to me. The few that bothered to find out simply dismissed it as more of a personal idiosyncrasy than a medical condition. Meanwhile my physical body and mind precipitously declined as evidenced by the lack of coordination and constant fatigue I experienced.

The situation was further compounded when I sought a medical attention at a company recommended clinic. The doctor I was assigned to failed to diagnose my ailment and rather than admitting this, he repeatedly told me on several occasions that I was afflicted by a "viral infection" regardless of the type of issue, like or nagging muscle stiffness which he would suggest that maybe I stretch out more and suggest that that was a symptom of the "virus" – but viral terminology I am told by those in the medical field is the equivalent of "I do not know what is going on!" What was particularly puzzling about this doctor was his reluctance to give me a referral, but instead came up with weird diagnosis as "viral infection" or "West Nile Virus" or "the Mississippi fungus", to name a few. In retrospective I should have requested to see another doctor because as I will show later this ailment became serious and almost cost me my life.

To alleviate some of the social and work-related challenges I confronted, I decided to go out and socialize with family and friends. I have always liked basketball since High School days and so I thought buying season tickets to the Minnesota Timberwolves would be a perfect fit. The problem I faced, though, was that due to my social relationship with "Baby". I lost ties with my childhood friends I had earlier met while in college. Besides, my home town is 70 miles from my work place and that would be rather cumbersome in terms of driving. My sister Olivia lived in downtown Minneapolis, on the other hand, and I knew she liked hoops as we both grew up playing sports competitively for many years but I was not sure if she was available to go to games on a continual basis; but, like myself, she knew how fun it would be to watch the Timberwolves play with such stars as Kevin Garnett, Wally Szerbiak and Chauncey Billups.

We had some good times watching the Wolves as they had an awesome season. Olivia knew people and she was able to get me courtside seats for a game against the Washington Wizards, which showcased Michael Jordan and I was able to get on the jumbo-tron while he was shooting a free throw under the rim (that was cool!). Olivia was not able to get to every game, as I thought would happen but scalping the tickets was however not difficult. I found that I really liked scalping them as it brought the sales person in me and I met a lot of interesting people. Even though I did not have the same click of friends I once had, going to the basketball games tested my self-will to not go out to the spots in downtown Minneapolis, as well. I would blame "Baby" and her insecurities for taking so much of my prime time when I wanted to party with the people and mingle with the pretty ladies, but the Bible study I had begun, I believe, was shielding me from the perils of these activities, and also the study was affecting my moral and ethical aptitude to do these kinds of things and for that I was thankful for the Bible study I was receiving.

In addition to socializing with friends and family, I needed to get a prayer life or connection with a higher power to make sense of what was going on in my life and so I started going to church with my younger sister Olivia since she seemed to have a good church (First United Methodist Church in the cities) and had a personal relationship with God, herself. Additionally, one of the preachers on the pulpit was a man that I went to college with named Deaniel, which added to the inviting ambiance. The fellowship there was nice, but I really liked listening to the sermons because that was when the Bible was preached from. Immediately, when I heard the message I always had questions since that is how my mind had been developed up to that point with all my schooling, but the answers always were inconclusive and ultimately with 'in my/our opinion' or 'that is just what we believe', which left me asking more questions. While attending this church, nonetheless, I witnessed an incredible performance from a choir from Cape Town, South Africa named the Christian Explainers that touched my heart substantially and has continued since and so I purchased all of their music and donated happily to their ministry.

But the void was still there for me with Biblical answers, at church, and so I began looking at other churches which unfortunately had the same rhetoric and general opinions and answers to specific questions I had about scriptures. Coincidently, I met this person named Bob with whom I was working, who seemed to have an understanding about the Bible, and he seemed to be a sincere person. I decided to consult him for guidance about the word of God. My decision to seek his counsel, I believe, was most beneficial for me as the Bible and its stories became comprehendible and dynamic for me. Interestingly, his mission in life was to become a preacher and missionary just as his dad and many members of his family.

Subsequently, Bob began giving me a Bible study called 'Search for the truth', after work primarily, and when "Baby" began to notice changes with me because of this, she began to curse and swear at me more frequently and intensely, especially when I was studying the Bible alone. Nonetheless, my desire to know more and understand what was written in scripture continued, and for this, Bob would often come to my condo in Burnsville for Bible study. He was a devoted teacher and so he came on weekends with his wife, Angelina and son Peter to my house and I travelled to their house in St. Paul. God was giving me revelation upon revelation through our study which led to more and more questions that he answered with more scriptures and not with opinions.

Eventually I began to read the Bible for myself. I would take this knowledge to church and actively listen to what was said on the pulpit. I really liked that church and the people there, but answers to questions I had were highly ambiguous and more opinionated or not even addressed as things would be said and accepted as facts, without thought or Biblical discernment and this began to really turn me off from that place and so I moved on, but not permanently.

At times "Baby" would try and join me in church as she saw the hope growing in me through the Bible, but she would complicate things by making us arrive late for the start of service at church and wanting to be the first to leave afterwards. She would then try to give me one of her 'Bible studies' about how I should pity her because I was the cause of all the misery in her life and she would quote scripture out of context and then she would swear at me and throw some vulgarities into her spiel, I believe, trying to provoke me to do the same back to her and disqualify me with the newly found hope that was going on. Despite her continued disruptions in my life, I never succumbed to her pressures, but instead I learned to either internalize her unfounded accusations or simply decided not to take her seriously. Above all this, it became abundantly clear to me that the central key to understanding my challenges could be found in the Bible. Consequently, I would wake up at 3a.m to read the Bible when it was quiet. Over a time, this helped me memorize verses from the Bible, and more importantly I realized that since God makes no mistakes, He would guide me through the toxic social relationship I was experiencing and eventually lead me to whatever conclusion He had in stock for me.

Unrealistic and simplistic as my approach to social issues may sound, this positive approach to life in general gave me strength and courage to deal with other challenges I was confronted with such as: my deteriorating health which was compromised since I was always fatigued and my bones felt like they were frozen; finding energy in order to fulfill my obligations to work 50 hours a week at my full time job; overseeing my rental properties which involved driving back and forth for a distance of about 70 miles from where I was staying in the Twin Cities; in order to supplement my income I was refereeing basketball and soccer games; and above all this, I had to deal with the challenges of fatherhood following the birth of my first son in 2002.

I considered the birth of my son as an answer to my prayers since his birth was both God's gift to me and also an affirmation of my Kisoga (Uganda) traditions which strongly cherish and value the need to have many children in general and boys in particular through whom one's lineage is sustained. I was personally over whelmed and emotional at the thought of becoming a dad. However, given my poor health, my mind was at peace that there was an heir to follow in my footsteps in case the Lord called me home. I also naively thought that the birth of my son would help improve my deteriorating social relationship with "Baby". On the contrary, although she realized that the baby was a bundle of joy, she carefully manipulated the situation in such a way as to use him as her security for me to accept and love her unconditionally. Rather than be confrontational with her, I internalized my anger and instead accentuate such positive accomplishment going on in my life such as: the birth of my son; good relationship with my family and the few friends I still had; enjoying the decent profits which were coming out of my rental property in my home town; and the purchase of a beautiful home in the Twin Cities.

Aside from the toxic social relationship I experienced, my overall productivity and energy were compromised by the continuing poor health I confronted. I was always awakened by "Baby" at 3a.m every day and remained awake until I left for work at 5a.m. Just going to and coming home from work were toiling on my body. Sitting up while driving and then walking up the stairs once I got home to disgruntled "Baby" was fatiguing. Subsequently, I took my medical problems to a clinic in the "Twin Cities" which as before was diagnosed my problem as a "viral infection". By February 2003, my stomach was not just growling coupled with running stool, but I could not hold dawn any food. Naturally I lost a lot of weight quickly, which was over 75+ lbs to be exact. Despite my failing health, the attending doctor would not give me a referral to go to a hospital. It was not until my parents and my brother Arthur confronted him then he referred me to another hospital where a competent doctor methodically diagnosed my illness as being allergic to gluten in foods. Interestingly before being diagnosed I continued to eat the foods that were making me ill once I was in the hospital and I collapsed on the bathroom floor where the doctor found me and figured out what was ailing me.

Things transpired very rapidly in February of '03. 'Baby' did not seem concerned that I was hospitalized or aware that I was so sick until the latter part of my hospital stay. She came to my room with my son after I was there for almost a week. I was reinvigorated after seeing his face and so I hurriedly discharged myself after the doctor in the hospital figured out what was making me so sick. Before I left, the doctor prescribed a very high dosage of prednisone steroids and told me I should have died of malnutrition with what was going on and emphasized the necessity of adherence to his words. He also gave me some medical metadata and told me that this type of ailment is usually found in people of Northern Europe and not sub-Saharan Africa. In private my dad told me that if we were in Africa they would have wrote this episode off as witchcraft.

In disbelief with the reality that I should have died, I hurriedly returned to work. I was jittery and not fully healthy and had PTSD. I did this because I did not want to stay at home with "Baby" and argue over nothing as I was taking medication. I regained 60 lbs after a week and I rushed back to work and I noticed that there were a few people who cared to find out what happened to me despite the anemic and weakly state I was in. This was a big corporation but everyone generally knew everyone else in the department where they worked. But what was puzzling to me is that people at work had the same attitude towards me as before I was hospitalized. Indeed, I was not looking for a "pity party", but with the advertisements these corporations made about how great they are, the least one would expect is that they put a human face to their policies. What I felt was strange about this company was that when in 2004 they decided to lay off people from the company they initially wanted to give me a lesser severance package that was different from what they had given to others! Amidst all this chaos I experienced, I neither had a personal advocate nor did I consult with an attorney conversant with job related cases. I was overwhelmed and in disbelief with the gravity of what happened to me and thought rusting the system would provide the necessary closure and healing that I needed. I also was still ailing from the nagging in my body and I knew there was something else still going on. But I did not want to be around doctors misdiagnosing me like the initial doctor as that was very stressful. But I still wondered; would I have a viable case against the company I was working for? How about a case against the doctor who several times diagnosed my illness as "viral infection", refused to give me a referral, did not recommend I use an ambulance to go to the referral hospital 40 miles when I was ill, but instead left me to drive as he was giving mixed messages? I think the answer is most probably yes!

But then I ask myself; why did I not file for divorce with the toxicity in the social relationship I was faced with? I could give several explanations as to why this never took place, but at the center of all this was my strong belief in epiphany – that is "It is God who decides the end from the beginning" (Isaiah 46 verse 10) and how He brings together and does not separate us (Matthew 19:26). Thus in addition to the inspiration from the birth of my son and the family ties, my new love of the Gospel kept me strong.

As I noted earlier, the process leading to my transformation to the centrality of religion in my life developed slowly, but steadily. To make sense out of what was going on in my life, I started to attend First United Methodist Church with my young sister Olivia. However, through a workmate (Bob) and Bible study, I started attending the Apostolic Church. My life and walk with the Lord changed at this time. What I enjoyed most about this new church is their strict scriptural interpretation of the Bible. In this church, I met men and women who had given their lives to preaching and teaching the gospel. In addition to Bible School learning this church brought in highly enlightened scholars who is addition to inspiration demonstrated their clear understanding of the gospel in the Bible. So influential has this church been that I was rebaptized (although first time I was baptized as an infant) by being immersed in water. I was ecstatic about this new baptism since I was now born again. To further fully understand the teachings of this church, I went to school at a local bible college where I received an Associate of Arts in Theology between 2005 and 2007. The totality of this religious belief has permeated every aspect of my life.

CHAPTER 4

Working in the Real-Estate Business: 2004-2007 – Challenges of Learning the Art of the Industry; Continuing Poor Health; Problems of Managing Rental Property and Second Trip to Ghana

Following my lay off in 2004, I was hired by a mortgage company. The immediate challenges I faced included: my lack of knowledge about the mortgage business; the fact that the job was 100% commission which technically meant that if one did not produce, one would not earn anything; the lack of benefits which was critical for me given my poor health; and the lack of training provided to new employees. For example, the first day I reported at work, I was introduced to my colleagues, but soon after many of them went back to their offices and got busy closing deals and getting paid.

The few that opened up to me told me that the central requirement in this business was the need for one to connect up with realtors. Immediately, I started to market myself by going around meeting people and my handing out my business cards. Unfortunately, my initial experience was unpleasant because some of the established agents showed either little interest or none at all working with me. My initial feeling was that sadly racism was well and alive in 2004. However, as time went by I realized that the cut throat competition in this business was such that one could say the guiding philosophy in this business was: "Everybody for himself and God for us all." As a Christian, I was somewhat bothered by this selfishness, but also realized that this was the reality of this "wicked world we live in".

In addition to being a loan's officer, I also trained to get a license as an agent. This was an ambitious plan in that one had to spread oneself out in order to meet one's obligation. Indeed, I collected the commission for both positions, but the process was somewhat cumbersome and time consuming.

One other approach I found beneficial was the need to establish good personal relationship with customers. I tried as much as I could to learn certain initial phrases in other languages. If there is one cultural achievement I made out of this industry, it was meeting people and learning bits and pieces in their languages. I, of course, did not learn the language in depth, but what was critical was starting on a good note with one's customer. A case in point was one agent I met at a real estate office. When I picked the business card at this office my attention gravitated toward one of the cards which had an African name. I requested and was granted permission to see this African realtor. His office was inoculate and when he stepped out co meet me, he was dressed in an expensive suit and wore shoes that were custom made. He looked intelligent and when he shook my hand, it appeared as though he has taken life out of me. I felt irrelevant to him and so to break the ice, I asked him if he was an Igbo from Nigeria. He immediately loosened up and began to talk freely about business. This was the beginning of a business relationship I established with a successful agent and lasted for the years I worked at the loan origination company. When I indicated to him that I would help his business as a loan officer, his answer was simple, namely: "If you refer me a deal, then I will refer you one."

A few days after I met this African realtor, he shocked me by giving me a referral on a veteran loan that would close in 60 days. I was excited to be entrusted with such a major responsibility. At the same time, I was nervous that this was probably a way of testing my competence. What even further made me fearful was the fact that this was a VA loan and like other government loans (FHA) it was to be scrutinized carefully. With that in mind, I methodically reviewed the paperwork that were submitted to me and raised all the relevant professional questions that were needed. So thorough was my review that some of my friends in the company felt I might have antagonized others in the process. Fortunately, those who made the final decision were impressed by what I did.

The closure of the deal heightened my confidence. I continued to market myself to whomever I met including clients from the USA and foreign nationals from Kenya, Nigeria, Cambodia, Vietnam, Cameroon, Ghana and Uganda, just to name a few. The total cultural experience I got immersed into with people from different countries was tremendous. I thus tried to put a human face to business and educational rewards were reflected in my ability to learn greetings from different languages. The financial rewards were just as good as the cultural ones since I personally owned four homes worth Over $175,000 in equity and I had a line of credit worth $60,000 for my rental properties in my home area.

However, my experience at this company was not a bed of roses, particularly after 2005. Cash was still flowing for me as people continued calling me non-stop to do business. The first indication of what true real estate business emerged when I realized that due to increased expenses the profits I was making from real-estate were being spent faster than before. This slowdown in business started late 2005 and continued into 2006 until the real-estate collapse 2007-2008. Part of the explanation was that everybody in the business was trying to play multiple roles – being a loan officer and a real-estate agent as well. There was also a relaxation in lending which in turn meant that individuals got loans they would otherwise have not received if strict policies were enforced. The overall impact of this was the loss of confidence in the market and lender hesitancy to do the same loans as before.

The slowing down of business meant in turn that the checks were not as sizable as they were before. By mid 2006 I was working 10 to 15 times as hard to make 1/3 of the money I was making a few months earlier. As home values plummeted, there was increased foreclosure, too.

This negatively impacted me since I was just not a loan's officer but I also owned some homes. I put up my two recently purchased properties in the twin cities on the market in an attempt to liquidate them since I could no longer sustain them from my meagre real-estate earnings.

Like other investors who wanted to make money when the real-estate was hot, I also owned rental properties. By spreading myself out rather too thin I became one of the victims of the real-estate demise. The rental properties were problematic on several fronts – they were 70 miles away from where I was living and this presented the problem of supervision from a far and the situation worsened since my poor health made it rather cumbersome to visit the properties as regularly as it would have necessitated. Consequently, I hired a management company to look after my properties. The problem I soon realized with the company I hired was that it was either incompetent, malicious or both. The company failed to do such minimum duties as: collecting rent and giving it to me; carry out minor apartment repairs as they occurred; did not respond to city code violations as it was supposed to; and treating tenants humanly. As one would expect, tenant turnover was high and so I had to use my personal funds to pay toward the mortgage I owed on these units. The company sent me exorbitant invoices of work that was never done at the units too.

With the help of a lawyer, I sued the company and was awarded judgment. The only problem was that these properties had been trashed that the money I got could hardly cover the cost of the repairs needed to update the properties. Indeed, the major repairs were done, but given the overall national economic decline which negatively impacted my earnings from real-estate, I had no choice but to hand in these properties to foreclosure in 2009.

Given the economic, health issues and lingering PTSD, I was confronted with, one would assume that one's spouse would provide comfort and overall support to me. To the contrary "Baby" remained as obstructive as ever. Instead she was more preoccupied with fulfilling her world's pressure than making long-range plans for the family. For example, soon after I was laid off from an Insurance Company in 2004, she insisted that we hold a big church wedding involving the invitation of her relatives from Africa and Europe. Staging such a wedding would be a financial disaster given that I did not have a job at the time. There was also the philosophical issue of whether this is the person I would like to spend the rest of my life given the turbulent relationship I had experienced with this individual! Putting my destiny in God's hands and strongly believing that as a Christian a church wedding would be appropriate thing to do, I consented to "baby's" wishes. The wedding was theatrical in that all kinds of her relatives who were flamboyantly dressed came. Perhaps the highlight of this drama was when "Baby" hysterically cried as she walked down the aisle toward the alter! Naturally, those who attended the ceremony were perplexed by the unusual situation. Once the festivities were over, everything went back to the previous chaos. The family bickering was well and alive. The birth of my second son in 2005 brought temporary happiness and unity but evaporated almost as soon as it appeared. Also, I must point out that I missed a trip to Uganda at this time for the wedding of my sister her husband; 'Baby' would have probably thought I was looking for a ride there which would have caused much unnecessary friction and I did not want to bring irregularity on the pregnancy.

To help me deal with this never-ending confusion, I turned to the Word of God, for spiritual therapy. Since I had more free time and some little cash, I wanted to take my hunger to learn more about scripture by enrolling in 2005 at a local Bible College. I knew that God was opening a door for me to take my talents into a different direction. Personally, I was deeply fascinated with the Old Testament and all the types and shadows it has pointing to Jesus Christ and His sacrifice at Calvary. The scholars at this college were both scholarly and exciting to listen to. Their teaching was powerful and brought transformation to me. Some of the scholars were so knowledgeable that instead of using the traditional textbooks most professors use, they used the Bible as the only source. This was refreshing for me because it gave a chance to students to look at the primary source, as opposed to secondary information in textbooks which in some cases is so editorialized as to weaken the original message from the Bible. I also enjoyed my classes because there were many non-traditional students, the majority of whom had a singleness of purpose for going back to school. Classes were also convenient for me since they ended at 1:00pm and thus made it possible for me to attend to other responsibilities. Thus, all in all going to a Bible College was enlightening and therapeutic for me in light of the many challenges I was confronted with at that time.

However, during the later months of 2006 I became convinced that I could not live with a façade of blissful peace with "Baby" constantly antagonizing me, coupled with my crumbling real estate empire and my continued ill health. The stress became so much that I felt that I had to travel outside the USA.

I still had some money put aside from my refinances and I started to think about my children enjoying the beauty that is elsewhere, as opposed to just seeing the miseries in my household. While I thought that this was a good idea, the problem was whether "Baby" would sign off on it. My suggestion to visit either Uganda or Europe was turned down, but she was receptive to visiting Ghana again. I concurred with her choice because Ghana is a place I wanted to see again or even retire. Additionally, Ghana was preparing to celebrate 50 years of independence in March of 2007 and the energy and national pride was going to be strong since it was the first independent Sub- Saharan African country. I purchased the air tickets in 2006 and made sure that before our departure I informed members of our church that we were travelling to Ghana particularly since we have missionaries around the world. I also wanted to know how I could get connected with our missionaries and Church in Ghana. I was given the contact information about our missionaries in Ghana. I was also given the address for their Church. Indeed, this was one side of Ghana I definitely wanted to explore.

Things were a little ambiguous prior to our take off in that "Baby" only provided a name and a P.O. Box address for her aunty as contact information for my parents. Although I was a grown man, my sickly past/ present with my hospitalization from my food allergy raised their concern. Thus, before boarding the plane for Ghana, my mom had a one-on-one discussion with "Baby" about making sure I was taken care of.

My children had never flown on a plane and I therefore enjoyed watching the looks on their faces as we took off and were flying in the clouds. After hours of flying, however, the excitement for them simmered as they wanted to land. My thoughts were on my 1st trip to Ghana in 1997 and I could not wait to step foot in the land again. When we were approaching Accra, the pilot announced that we would be landing at Kotoka Airport momentarily. Immediately, I saw many people on the plane stand up shake hands and say 'akwaba' like I previously observed. This was peaceful and I felt like I was at home, much like my first trip. I could see that "Baby" also was excited to be back in her country, as well. Finally, we landed at Kotoka Airport in Accra, Ghana. After we had made it through customs with our luggage, we were jubilantly welcome by "Baby's" relatives.

Things were busy and hectic in Accra and especially as we drove to go to the residence where we stayed. We were heartily welcomed and our luggage was taken to the guest chambers of the daycare owned by "Baby's" aunt. I immediately took refuge in my room with the boys since we needed to rest from the time difference and jet lag.

Out of natural happiness to be home, "Baby" was busy chatting with her family most of the time. In fact the first days of our visit we were introduced to nieces, nephews, aunties, uncles, etc. It was great to meet all these people and also to get reintroduced to African culture in general and Ghanaian culture in particular. The remarkable thing I noted was that although I have used western terminology (uncle) to refer to "Baby's" relatives, among many African societies such terms are not used. For example, in many African societies it will be discriminatory if you referred to your "step-sister" as "step-sister" instead you simply refer to her as "sister". It was unfortunate that my sons could not understand all this since they were young. Some of the people who came to meet us briefed us about the church whereabouts and Sunday activities. "Baby" was surprised to see that I got along with many people. It became apparent to her to learn that Ghana had more to offer to the world beyond the traditional tourist sight-seeing. Ghanaians have a deep history with the west and church revival with Christianity and so that took the burden away of me being perceived as a "weirdo" or a "Jesus freak"!

No one seemed to be surprised therefore that I wanted church and a lot of it. Unfortunately, "baby" had a different agenda. I think she wanted to show her friends or people that knew her in her prior life how far she has advanced. Many of her acquaintances had their own businesses and were hustling to get ahead in life. These women also had children but were not married or living with the father of their children. When "Baby" took me and the boys to these women's business, I immediately could detect the rancor and resentment they had towards her. Their looks seemed to ask me if I knew what kind of girl "Baby" was! Strangely, it was the same reaction people showed to "Baby" when she visited other places in the capitol city Accra and other cities. Many of the places such as the slave castles were not new to me since I had visited them during my last trip to Ghana in 1997. My visit to Kumasi was somewhat, though, newer and special on several fronts: this is "Baby's" father's place of birth where I had the opportunity to visit her dad; Kumasi is also historically important since it is the seat of the royal kings of the Ashanti people who put up a fierce resistance to stop the British colonization of Ghana; and I also enjoyed the trip to Kumasi because of the young children I met who touched my heart. These kids reminded me of the angels who blessed my heart in 1997. These kids all knew I was with a Ghanaian girl as they approached me and introduced themselves. Among other things they told me they were attending school and briefly outlined what they may end up doing when done with school. Initially, I thought these were "con people" in the making. However, as I listened to them more I became convinced that these were kids with potential to do anything, if the right opportunities were offered to them. I gave them some money and advised them to work hard and believe in the good Lord. Honestly, I was flustered as my emotions took me back to the children I met on my first trip to Ghana in 1997.

As refreshing as the trip to Ghana was, I ran into old challenges, the most of which was my deteriorating health. I had low energy and Ghana's hot and humid weather made matters worse. They were times I would sweat profusely that I could not walk long distances and in some cases I was concerned that I could collapse due to dehydration or over exhaustion. "Baby's" unpredictable behavior exacerbated the situation on a number of occasions. One case in point was when we went to a grocery store to pick items for our house use. The crux of the matter came when we came to pay for the items we picked. I had forgotten to go and exchange dollars into cedes (the local currency) and so I expected that since it was a small amount of money "Baby" could pay. When I requested her to do this, she glared at me and spoke to me in a confrontational way using a local language I could not understand because of the use of slang. Based on the reaction on the faces of those who understood the language and slang, it is apparent that she was using vulgar language. Out of politeness and in keeping with my policy of internalizing challenges, I pretended as though all was well.

I also found peace and comfort in reading the Bible and attending church services. As I earlier noted, I requested my "home church" in the USA to connect up with its representative in Ghana. I very much wanted my children to accompany me to this church service, but "Baby" was not enthusiastic about it. Consequently, I went alone to the service. Following my introduction to the congregation, the music, dance, and preaching followed. All my problems ranging from my toxic social relationship, to slowly crumbling real-estate empire, came to a standstill as the music and praying took on the therapeutic role I was reenergized as the fellowship and comradery intensified. At the end of the service, tears of joy ran down my face. But then sadness came over me as I realized that my children could not experience this phenomenon with me. After service, I fellowshipped by meeting new friends. I attended other church services and they were as therapeutic as ever.

However, as time went by I realized that my health was deteriorating fast as evidenced by the rapid loss of weight. I, therefore, expressed to "baby" my desire to return to the USA for medical treatment. Indeed, my rapidly declining weight is what almost killed me years earlier from gluten-loaded diet and she knew how rapidly things worsened for me back then. She could also deduce when I asked her to direct me to a medical person for the evacuation because I just was not enjoying myself anymore. Initially my tickets were for a 4 week stay in Ghana which would have included the new year of 2007, but after 2 weeks I wanted out because of my ailment and personal matters that I eluded to. The medical liaison thus issued a medical evacuation note for me, nonetheless. But our departure would not be until after Christmas. Christmas was uneventful and lonely for me. There were several people there that "baby" did not bother to introduce me to and I did not go out of my way to meet them because I just wanted to leave. I kept quiet, nonetheless, and within 2 days, we were departing. I had seen and done what I wanted to and I knew that I most probably would never step foot in this beautiful country again.

Finally, we were off and departing. I had mixed emotions because as an adult I had built up such a deep fondness about Ghana, but now I wanted nothing to do with this place with "Baby" in the picture. I did not want to leave this place with such feelings, however. I reminded myself that this country was not my original place of birth, but I was adopted into it both by Ghanaians in Africa and in the states. I also reflected on the tremendous ministering and therapy I received at Church and what that did for me. To complicate matters for me, I could not stop thinking about all the senseless arguments and confrontations during this trip with "Baby". I knew that my silence was my only defense to her attitude and living in the states I had some security, as well.

We had a safe trip to the USA, but reality soon set in – I had bills from my rental business and all indications were that my real estate business had slowed down considerably. My consolation was that I would be around my family for the New Year. 2007 started on a good note for my family since my older sister Monica gave birth to a handsome baby boy. Despite the slowing down of the real estate business, I stuck to my guns and continued to do what I had done in the past. After a quite 2007 January, I got a good lead and a loan was approved for the applicant. I was happy about this transaction since I collected a sizable check. This was probably the last major earning I made in 2007. I made some infrequent refinances but I was hardly making any money from my rentals. By November 2007 it was clear that I needed to supplement my income in order to keep afloat.

Thus, I started looking for part-time work with a focus of establishing a career in sales since I had enjoyed that experience in real estate. I very much like a job which involved interaction with people. I had friends in telecommunication who were making good money and were working just part time by selling mobile phones. I started applying to several companies. I also was introduced to a gold and silver coin shop, but I was turned off because of their poor benefits. I continued looking elsewhere until I was offered a part-time job at telecommunications company in 2007. This started a new chapter in my life which involved working with a telecommunication company between 2007-2011.

CHAPTER 5

Working at a Telecommunication Company, 2007-2011: Benefits and Challengs

Getting this job was timely not just because I could now get additional income, but also because of other advantages I got. Since I was working part-time, the new job enabled me to continue working in the real-estate business. The flexible nature of the job also helped me to deal with family issues such as finding time to take my boys out to the park, which were becoming more and more precious as they were getting bigger. The added advantage of this job was its proximity to the place where I was living and the excellent personality of the manager who hired me. Unlike my previous experience and other managers I later worked with at this company, he was humane in his business dealings with other employees. Aside from being professional, he was friendly and generally sympathetic to the plight of others. This manager's attitude more than anything else greatly impressed me and energized me to work enthusiastically for the company.

Additionally, the company offered decent benefits such as: dental and health insurance which became immediately available as soon as I started working; encouraged workers to go for unlimited commission; provided 401K retirement investment for employees; and being a Fortune 500 company, one had the opportunity for upward mobility – something that I personally valued given the educational qualifications I had.

However, the job had draw backs such as: the salary was much lower than my previous jobs; there was also quota sale required of every employee; when I started working full-time at two other stores, I ran into the challenges of driving into congested traffic; and the mediocre managers I later worked with once I became a full-time worker. For example, I got awkward vibes from one of the manager when the first thing he asked me in private was if I wanted to look for a different job! When I ignored his unsolicited advice, he would write me up on frivolous things with the objective of discouraging me.

These challenges notwithstanding, I continued working as diligently as I could in part because I desperately needed money to pay my bills, but also because several friends I made at the store told me that this was unfortunately the nature of "corporate America." My situation would not have been as desperate as it turned out if "Baby" had stepped up to pay some of the bills. Although she had lived in the USA for almost 10 years and was working full-time, she would have none of my requests to pay some bills. Consequently, I was forced to dip into my IRA to pay for regular house bills.

I would probably have weathered this economic challenge if it were not for my poor health which followed me like my shadow. My health took a turn for the worst when I collapsed on June 8, 2008. On arrival at work on that day, I found my energy to be low and so I sat down and drank a caffeinated drink with the hope that this would remedy the problem. Unfortunately, this did not help much since I could not multitask or concentrate well during the first couple of hours.

My body started to uncontrollably shake and I felt that I needed to rest for about 5 minutes. Consequently, I spoke to the team leader I was working with and I indicated that I needed to take a 5 minute break in the back room since I was shaking and my hands were swelling up. Within seconds, the shaking and swelling got worse and I was incoherent as I walked by the team leader heading to the back room. Although I was already profusely shaking and swelling up when I walked by him, he did not pay much attention to my situation. As time went by, my teeth were violently chattering and I also became disoriented as I passed by him. Uncharacteristically, he continued talking to customers while in actual fact he was usually expected to be doing some other stuff for the company in the back room. As I sat down in the back room, I realized that my body was unsettled. Conversely my shaking worsened as I slouched on the chair and yelled out for help at the top of my voice several times because I felt like I was passing out. I could hear him chatting with the customers that he just met, but he did not respond to me. I wanted to call an ambulance on my phone which was in my pocket, but I fell out of my seat when I tried to reach in my pocket since I was using my arms to sit upright on the chair. I was desperate and screaming for help! Why could he not hear me as I was pleading for help, I wondered to myself? I also thought that there was supposed to be two people in every place at all times to avoid accidents like this?

Regardless of the team leader's inattentiveness to my pleas in the backroom, my shaking intensified as I sat on the floor which was becoming comfortable that I just I wanted to just shut my eyes and take a nap. I was distressed and shaken to the core since I was afraid I could die. My breathing had slowed down substantially and my life seemed to flash before me. I could not move my body and I did not know how much time elapsed as I was out. I thought that I was dead as all my senses seemed to have shut down. Regardless of this fact, nobody heard my non-stop pleas for help. Nobody saw me fall over and pass out besides the cameras in the backroom. In fact, I thought nobody their even cared. I was, though, consoled to realize that there were cameras everywhere in the backroom at The telecommunications office recording this event and so my family would have a rough idea as to what had happened to me as I thought I was going to make my final resting place on the ground alone. As helpless as I laid on the floor, my mind kept wondering what would happen to my boys if I were to pass on!! Yes, they had a mom, but one who I had no confidence in as I have demonstrated in the fore going pages. I also kept preoccupied with the possibility of my dying without leaving behind a daughter I wanted to name Robina Priscilla Mpayenda – names that would have recognized my late Auntie Robina Mugweri and my mom's maiden name Mpayenda.

Suddenly, as these thoughts were flashing before me, somebody began scrapping me off of the floor while I was losing my life in the backroom. This was now my graveyard, I thought. As it turned out, this was a police officer who was the 1st responder. He checked my vital signs, found a pulse, and hauled me over his shoulder and carried me out to an ambulance. It was dark out outside and I do not know how much time elapsed because it was light out when I went to the backroom at Telecommunications office. I could see, nonetheless, that the team lead looked bewildered since he was still there talking to the people he had met when I went to the back room. I saw a swarm of flashing lights when I got outside of the building. There were several police officers and ambulances because of my collapsing and I felt uncomfortable. The people in the ambulance immediately scrambled once they saw how despondent my situation was and they put me on an IV to keep me alive. They also checked my temperature and it was 104 degrees! Thus I got into the ambulance and they rushed me to Hospital.

The hospital did not move me to a room immediately because they could not verify my health insurance without my card. I called my parents and told them what happened to me and the predicament I was in at the hospital. As concerned parents, my mom and dad drove in the middle of the night and got my card to the hospital. Once I got the insurance card, I was moved to a nice room and was given food and a drink. As I laid in my hospital bed, I reflected on my life with regard to my health issues I had encountered over the years, particularly when I was hospitalized in 2003 because of the gluten ailment. Fortunately, my parents were present and provided emotional comfort and support as I was trying to make sense of what had happened to me. Additionally, I read the Bible while I was waiting for the doctors to carry out the tests.

The initial diagnosis of what caused me to collapse was that it was a bacterial infection caused by an insect. This initially sounded plausible to me given that I had taken my boys to the parks and possibly was bitten by an insect. However, on second thoughts I was doubtful if this diagnosis was just as wrong as the one made by a doctor in 2003 when my gluten intolerance problem was erroneously diagnosed as a "viral infection."

Just before doctors could discharge me from the hospital, a Russian woman entered my room and identified herself as a licensed private practicing neurologist. Her appearance was stoic and almost militaristic which I thought was somewhat intimidating. I, though, felt comfortable with her at first because I was becoming conversational in the language of Russian. After a brief introduction, she told me I have multiple sclerosis or MS. She insisted that I meet with her immediately because I have lesions in my brain that I needed to medicate! She said in no uncertain words that this an injury to my brain that will only get worse unless I immediately tend to it. She therefore wanted to meet me at her office straightaway to recommend what I should do to manage this disease. After hearing her words, I knew that this woman was no nonsense! Her eye contact and demeanor was very intense much like the doctor who diagnosed me with celiac in 2003 after my collapse in the bathroom at the hospital.

Rather than accept her diagnosis, I started getting into a soliloquy and self-denial! Who was she to tell me this, I defensively and foolishly thought? What exactly is an injury to my brain like MS, I also thought? I immediately remembered someone I met at The telecommunications office who told me that MS was not a 'viral infection'. When did this MS start? Maybe she made an error, I also foolishly thought? What was further frightening was her insinuation that I not only should I probably stop working at The telecommunications office, but I had to end all my professional aspirations to concentrate on the treatment of this disease. My parents were just as perplexed and flabbergasted as I was to hear this recommendation from the doctor. I further refused to accept this as the correct diagnosis because aside from the overall fatigue I was experiencing, I felt that on the whole I was well enough to continue working.

After being hospitalized for about a week, I was discharged and received a joyous welcome by my two sons. They gave me hugs and said they missed me. While my oldest son was concerned by my overall sickly appearance, the youngest wanted me to take them to the park. "Baby" pretended as if she did not see me and continued on with her endless phone talking with her friends. Her expression on the face indicated that I was an unwanted person who she was ready to fight with. She neither bothered to visit me in hospital nor did she call. In my characteristic way, I internalized all this advance reaction to my return and pretended all was well with me. The consolation I got from her reaction to my 2008 illness was that unlike my 2003 gluten illness, she did not tell me to my face that she wished I had died!

The toxic social problems in my home were further increased by the grim financial situation I was in. On checking my mail, I came across many bills that needed payment, including the astronomical ambulance bill that was related to my hospitalization. My rental property was practically non-existent due to the failure by renters to pay their dues and the poor management that became worse following my sickness. The real estate business had become so excruciatingly slow that when I called some of my main contacts to try to initiate something their numbers were either disconnected or no one knew their whereabouts. In other words, my only source of income was my meagre pay from The telecommunications office following my injury them.

Before I went back to work, I had a follow up appointment with the doctor who also diagnosed me with MS. I am grateful that my parents took off time from their busy schedule and accompanied me to see the doctor. She first explained to me that MS is a traumatic brain injury. She also said that this disease was relapsing and remitting for me. She then emphasized that I needed to start with medication, physical therapy and recommended that I could start with a drug like prednisone which is a powerful medication that cost $5000 a dosage. She then explained the debilitating nature of this disease and told me what it could do to my ability to walk, my coordination, my ability to button shirts, to name a few. She noted that my ability to work would most probably be greatly compromised or even inhibited because of this ailment. She emphatically noted that I would need to pay attention to the treatment of this disease. To emphasize the severity of what she discovered, the doctor also recommended that I engage in physical therapy to help me manage the side effects of this disease. She meticulously continued to describe what this disease was doing to my body. She also pointed out some medical meta-data that finds that this disease like celiac when I was diagnosed usually affects people in the Northern hemisphere and not people from my demographic (which is true probably because of the complexity and cost to diagnose it in areas I hail from, even though brilliant medical minds come from such areas. Both my parents and I were taken aback by her extensive specificity with this disease. She also had all authority, as a licensed neurologist, to recommend that I step away from my job. In a nutshell, she told me that MS is a condition that will follow me around everywhere and could limit my personal vocational mobility. My parents and I were taken aback in disbelief in hearing all this as it pertained to me.

Despite her impeccable qualifications and the excellent methodical approach she used in analyzing my situation, I still had lingering questions related to her overall conclusions. Among the many questions I still had were: Is it possible her diagnosis was as off like the doctor who mis-diagnosed my gluten illness in 2003 as "viral infection"? How do you explain the view that if MS generally afflicts people of European descent, it attacked me who is an African? Granted that I have MS, what evidence is there to demonstrate that all what she predicted will happen to me, particularly if I use the medication she recommended to use? Thus overwhelmed by these unsolved questions in my mind, instead of inquiring into the permanency or impermanency of her discovery on my physicality or aspirations, the only question I raised to the doctor at my second meeting with her was "could I get a second opinion about what she had suggested?" My parents and the doctor were baffled that I raised this question. Consequently, my parents insisted that I start taking the medication as prescribed by the doctor.

In hindsight, it was foolhardy on my part either to question the doctor's diagnosis or taking it lightly at best. This attitude of mine was more dangerous than the earlier actions I was engaged in my life namely: swimming in the shark-infested Atlantic Ocean during my first trip to Ghana in 1997 and my decision on the same trip to break away from the rest of the group in order to venture out in the unknown streets of Ghana's capitol Accra in the dark. My early denial of MS had far-reaching ramifications because it made me make ill-advised decisions which I will probably regret for ever. I thought I was "superman" and therefore felt exercising would perhaps take care of my problems the doctor warned me of; but alas, this never happened! I tried working out as hard as I could, even though my body could not take it. Regardless of my stretching, my coordination was off as evidenced by the many falls I had in my attempt to play basketball. My general balance was off with everything and my fatigue increased after doing minimum physical activity.

Things got trickier and more complicated when I went back to work. Everything was awkward since everyone including the District Manager seemed to be looking at me as though I was an individual who should have died on June 8, 2008. No one including the manager did not ask me what happened or even acknowledged that I passed out in the back room. As I was working on an in-store project at a later point, moreover, my manager asked me to do some work, which included physical activity. When I told him that this would not be possible for me because I could not because I had MS; he then asked if that was diagnosed before or during my employment with the company? As soon as I told him it was during my employment with the company, he gave me a blank stare, smirked and his behavior changed 180 degrees as he just kept silent. I felt ashamed as my thoughts digressed to when I first met him and his paranoia that I would sue the company. I had no desire to just sue, but I realized that they had a fiduciary obligation to pay me for what happened to me on June 8th, 2008, much like I believe the previous company I worked for had the same obligation to compensate me for my gluten hospitalization in February of 2003. The insurance was paying for my $5000 a month drug and with my PTSD, I thought that would be suffice as I thought to myself confusingly.

To finalize this shell shock of events for me from June 8th of 2008, my team leader came to me as I was leaving for lunch one day and he advised me that I needed to sue the company. I think he may have seen the video recording of the event. But with all my PTSD and remorse from the day of the event and the time that elapsed from the occurrence I could not understand why I should do such an adversarial thing. However, as soon as I wanted to speak more with him about his suggestion to me, he was let go. I thought I was the cause of his departure because he advised me that I should sue the company because of what happened to me on June 8th of 2008 in the backroom. I am fairly sure today that there was probably something else going on with him and the company. Notwithstanding this fact I knew that Eddie was not an attorney. But his comment as a 2nd person who was concerned about what happened to me would have made him into an advocate for my situation, I believe. But instead of an advocate, the company left me to fend for myself from the events that aggravated me from June 8th of 2008 in the backroom.

After the team leader had left the company, no one at the store discussed the June 8th, 2008 incident or approached me to discuss my accident at the company and I therefore felt alone. I also began to feel deep resentment that my sickness on June 8th of 2008 at the company even brought such attention to me. I further confusingly felt remorse that I was diagnosed with MS on their watch especially after my encounter with my manager. Thus, I did my best to not show anyone how bothered I was by just smiling and making other people laugh. I also tried to convince myself that my MS diagnoses was a really bad 'viral infection' instead of the debilitating disease that the Russian women said it was. To convolute the matter for me the company brought in a new team leader and other employees who knew nothing about what happened to me. At this point, it was only perhaps my manager and the attorneys at the company who saw the video of my collapse on June 8th, 2008 and who knew what happened to me. The new people accepted my limping and struggling to move around as normal.

One subsequent afternoon, a seemingly odd occurrence happened to me at The telecommunications office when a man from WCCO evening news on channel 4 approached me. I thought he was a customer at the company looking to buy a phone or wanting to pay his bill. Thus, I was thinking more business for me or maybe even career advancement for me as he would have been a good lead and I was looking to move ahead in my career. But, he stopped and looked into my eyes inquisitively, then he asked me if there was something I wanted to tell him. His question was followed by a moment of awkward silence. I knew straightaway that he was refereeing to the incident on June 8th, 2008. Two company employees were standing behind me and when the person from WCCO news asked me this question. I tried not to show him any emotion, but my PTSD began to uncontrollably act up. June 8, 2008 was definitely a story for the news, but out of fear of losing my job with all my anxiety I said I had nothing to say. Basically, I know if I told WCCO channel 4 news my story about June 8th of 2008 at the company, I would have been contacted by attorneys who would have represented my rights and found a legal advocate. I say this because it probably would have been put on the evening news, and therefore, employment and personal injury attorneys would most probably let me know that I need to utilize their services to recover what was lawfully mine as a result. But as with the previous company from February of 2003, I did not scream foul but I just kept quiet and dealt with all the pain privately.

Immediately, following my interaction with WCCO channel 4 nightly news, I had an interaction with another person from KMSP channel 9 evening news. As with WCCO channel 4 I thought, this was my opportunity to network and move ahead with my career. I got into a nice conversation with him as we talked about one of the state colleges which was his almamater and where I received my MBA as well. His approach was laid back, but I was thinking he wanted me to tell him my story from June 8th of 2008. I sensed this is why he was there, but my PTSD was still on edge and I could not muster the courage to tell him what had happened to me. As with WCCO channel 4 evening news, he would also have become my advocate had I told him my story. But the pain and rejection from June 8th, 2008 at The telecommunications office was too recent for me coupled with my PTSD. Thus, I kept quiet as I did with WCCO Channel 4. Part of my problem was that I let several weeks elapse without consulting with an attorney about my June 8, 2008 illness. Due to the fact that I had no advocate at this company, much like I did not at the previous company, my PTSD further mounted and thus I was looking for any excuse to minimize the gravity and traumatization of what happened on June 8th, 2008.

Indeed, my story on the news would have changed the landscape of how I managed my collapse at the company on June 8th, 2008 and my diagnoses with MS, I believe as I probably would have retained an attorney and recovered my money in damages. But my PTSD kept me silent throughout and I wanted to believe I only had a 'viral infection' as I was diagnosed earlier by a doctor I consulted with at the clinic. Therefore, these news reporters told stories about calamities that happened to other people. But their headlines also gave a lot of attention to a dampening economy. The foreclosures were spiraling out of control and the trickle-down effect was tremendous. The president interceded nationally with financial bailouts and we were soon in a 'Great Recession'. But due to the fact that I kept my silence with my traumatic and newsworthy event at The telecommunications office on June 8th, 2008, this 'Great Recession' became 'the Great Viral Infection with MS' for me.

Not only did I stay faithful to the company, in the interim, after the traumatic incident for me, I did my best to distant myself from that day and erase the gravity of the event. The MS signs on my body were obvious, however. Regardless of this fact, I foolishly thought that time would heal the pain and trauma and even MS for me from what happened on that dreadful day of June 8th of 2008 at the company. I also thought that this company would support me and do the right thing, which would have been to recommend I stop working there, seek legal counsel, and focus on my MS and utilize my benefits that I was paying for. But with my PTSD, I was always anxious at the company after my collapse at the store because of June 8th of 2008. I was helplessly dragging my foot walking around the premises and setting up new phones and even just standing on my feet at the store was toilsome on my body. Buttoning my shirts and getting ready for work also became more difficult as my coordination was altered because of my MS, as the doctor told me. I faithfully paid on my insurance benefits at the company, throughout these tumultuous times for me and I smiled and acted like nothing was wrong as I was in self-denial. Even though I had mastered the art of smiling and joking my way through these tough times, things were getting rapidly more difficult for me as I was daily returning to the place I should have died in the back room of this company on June 8th, 2008. This was similar to when I was working at the previous company when I almost died in February of 2003. I was also taking my CoPaxone medication daily but the longer I was taking it, the more I forgot about what instigated it, which was my collapse at this company on June 8th of 2008.

Additionally, my manager, who most probably watched me pass out on the video several times but said nothing to me about it, held me up to the same monthly sales quota standards as the other employees at the store, which added pressure. I think he may have realized that since I had told him I have MS, I had limitations in my physical activities at work. Thus, he backed off the physical requirements for me. In essence, I think if I would partake in these activities and there was a simple fall that would magnify the liability that company was responsible to me for in addition to my collapse on June 8th, 2008. I would still stumble nonetheless and trip but I picked myself up and acted like there was something on the ground. I was still relatively healthy and the company kept a constant pressure on me and kept me on edge as I thought they would fire me if I did not make the quota. This worsened my PTSD and my instincts told me I had to prove I was perfectly healthy because I enjoyed challenges even though I was not well. Even though the limping and dragging of my foot became more obvious nobody at the company was saying anything to me about it, I thus started to believe I was getting healthier. Interestingly, the only people who said anything to me about my limping and dragging of my foot were people who worked in the area, one of whom was my sister Fida. At family functions, it was not noticeable because I was mostly seated and so it never really came up. People outside of work saw me limping around from a distance but not on a daily basis. They would make comments to me and ask if something was causing the abnormalities. But to hide the emotional pain, I would smile and say everything was fine. Besides these comments, no one attempted to advocate or even say anything to me who saw the stumbling on a daily basis. I therefore did my best to convince myself that it was only a bad and lingering 'viral infection'.

Five weeks after I had collapsed at the company, it was time for my 2nd MRI at the hospital to reconfirm what the specialist doctor had diagnosed. By this time, I was limping around and occasionally falling as I moved around to and fro. But without an advocate I convinced myself that it was that elusive 'viral infection'. I proceeded to go to the hospital by myself and I checked in. They proceeded to fasten me into a machine where I would go through the X-Rays. But at this point all I could think about was getting to work at the company on time and then taking my boys to the park afterwards. At this appointment, I did not meet with a neurologist and so I had to wait for about another 2 weeks to get my MRI results.

Basically, I had no advocate or union to turn to at the company, much like I did not at an insurance company. My PTSD was mounting and I was looking for any reason to justify that my MS ailment would leave me. I kept thinking about tricky viral infections from Park Nicollet the more my body hurt. I did research and I found millionaire celebrities like Richard Pryor, who is deceased, and Montel Williams who have this ailment. I further discovered from a distance how they were dealing with this disease. I would watch Williams on TV and I would see him walking around normally and smiling and advocating healthy eating, by juicing (which is good). Without knowing anything about his daily struggle with this disease, I presumed that since he is black as I am he did not have the same type of MS as everyone else. I thought his was a temporal 'viral infection' type of MS, like mine. But my inconclusive information I deduced only helped me to further disqualify the severity of this disease for me and the findings of neurologist. What I could not come to terms with surprisingly is that these men are very wealthy and I am not. Secondly, MS is a highly complex disease, like cancer, in that it does not affect two people in the same way. Based on my inconclusive data I had, therefore, I tried to foolishly prove my normalcy and disprove the brilliant medical neurologist I met with by eating more protein and drinking more healthy juices.

I continued my employment with the company while faithfully paying on my benefits in the interim. The more I worked in the store the more I felt like what happened to me on June 8th, 2008 did not really happen. Also, I felt that the brilliant subsequent words of the Russian born doctor were more of a bad dream than reality, despite the obvious signs of my sickness. But I soon got a call from the hospital from a brilliant Vietnamese woman neurologist and she also diagnosed me with MS, like the Russian doctor. She also gave me similar counsel like the first doctor. Despite all this, I still thought I had a viral infection and not MS. I was still working out and eating healthier and so I accepted the obvious physical impairments that were present as a really bad type of a 'viral infection'. I thought it was mixed in with my MS. Unlike my initial meeting with the first doctor, the second doctor asked me about my home life and living arrangements. Perhaps she asked this because MS is a life changing injury to the brain that warrants many accommodations both personal and vocational. Her question softened my heart and I would tell her that my living arrangements were fairly hostile. I appreciated her concern. At this point nonetheless, I disassociated this company as the responsible party for their negligence on June 8th, 2008. I foolishly thought that this was my 'viral infection' ailing me from the previous company days, which in reality it was from my hospitalization in February of 2003 as I worked there. In either case she eventually handed me off to another neurologist for reasons I was not certain of.

Time was not healing my MS as I thought it would. But I was losing control of my body as I still thought that the cause of my problems were largely due to 'viral infections' and not MS. My continual denial and my insistence on the 'viral infection' theory, was not helpful at all. I was noticeably limping around everywhere while I was working at this company and sometimes falling in pain. Subsequently, I told my new team leader that my feet and legs hurt me while I was at work walking around, but he told me to buy Dr. Scholl's shoe insoles. I knew he himself was a victim of a work-related accident, but he knew nothing about my ailment and I did not tell him either as my discomfort mounted. I just kept quiet about June 8th, 2008 at The telecommunications office as my PTSD starting with the insurance company. I thought that my silence was in The company 's and my best interest. I would only open up and tell people who would identify themselves as medical professionals, such as nurses and some doctors, on the other hand. But I would soon learn that the title nurse or even doctor did not necessarily qualify them as experts with my ailment as no one, in general, knew exactly just how debilitating this disease was but me or someone suffering from the disease.

On the home front, things were equally as volatile as I was adjusting to my new life with my MS. 'Baby' seemed to be always on her laptop using Google, as that was becoming the search engine of choice. At the same time, she seemed to be constantly yelling on her phone to her friends about what I thought were irrelevant and childish topics. But as long as the kids were not crying and she was not fighting with me, I did not pay attention to her. This was always my strategy with her, but this time I was obviously sick and receiving monthly medications that, I think, she knew I was taking. I say this because I would dispose of sealed containers full of used syringes in the trash. The name CoPaxone was on the empty boxes. I was not looking for just pity, but she could have easily deduced that this was most probably a result of the reason I was recently gone for a week. Google would have explained CoPaxone as a medication for people with MS. I think she could have put her phone down and asked me a few questions about it and inquired into when I was diagnosed with the disease and where I was, for that matter. Instead, she just made sure the mortgage was paid and later looked for a foolish disagreement to argue about with me as I struggled to get around. In essence 'baby' saw first-hand the degradation with my health over the years since my sickly days at the insurance company because of gluten in the food and now The telecommunications office on June 8th, 2008. But like most everyone who saw me almost die at the insurance company in February of 2003 or at The telecommunications office on June 8th of 2008 at The telecommunications office, she acted like nothing was wrong with me. Therefore with my PTSD worsening by the day, I also acted like nothing really happened.

Regardless of the general inattentiveness to my sickness at The telecommunications office and at my residence with 'baby', my sons remained my utmost priority. I continued to do everything in my power to keep them happy at all times as they were my therapy for my untreated PTSD from the insurance company and The telecommunications office. Even though they did not understand the gravity of my sickness, I took them to Church, the water/parks and registered them in athletic activities. Basically, part of me was living through them again. But as I tried to exert myself in activities that required minimal physical activities like walking to the water/parks or to soccer fields or basketball courts, excessive fatigue and discomfort took over my legs. Notwithstanding this fact, I continued to push myself, because no one told me anything was wrong with me and I was my own worst critique in thinking there was either.

As I pushed myself to shake off my 'viral infection' MS one Sunday afternoon, I decided to engage myself in a Church organized basketball game after service. It was not as competitive as some of the pick-up games I was used to, but there were some exceptionally good athletes there. One of those athletes was a nationally recognized player who coincidently attended the same high school that my sister Monica worked at. Lacing up my shoes on the same court with him reminded me how greatly I missed competitive basketball. I had stepped away from regularly playing basketball at this point, because of my recurring diagnosed 'viral infections', which was now the 'MS' type. Fortunately, those 'viral infections' did not bother me at first as all my years of playing the game brought my touch back, straightaway. But after only a few trips up and down the court, strangely, my legs froze up on me and I just wanted to sit down. I managed to barely walk the rest of the game, and I remembered the counsel from the Park Nicollet doctor who said that I just needed to stretch out more. Therefore, I sat down for some time and stretched a little and I felt a little better. However, as time went by, the MS effects became more pronounced on my body on several fronts, namely: waking up in pain and discomfort; needing eye glasses for daily use; stumbling and grimacing while walking; recurring muscle spasm as my hand writing becoming sloppy; and these conditions became more apparent as I tried to finish the game walking and as 2009 became a year of hobbling. My limping, tripping and falling frequently while trying to walk.

I began to socialize with everyone on the court after the game. I knew he would be playing division 1 basketball, but I knew that his high school was also elite for basketball. But as soon as I mentioned to him that my sister's name is Monica Konso, he looked at me emotionally as his eyes began to get glossy and he said to me respectfully that he knows Ms. Konso! Wow, I thought to myself, Ms. Konso? I know that my sister Monica has worked very hard to get to where she is, and her plight as a single mom with two young babies was a story all by itself. But the glossy eyes from this guy and for him to call her Ms. Konso with such reverence said something else to me!

As I thought on this situation, my overall reality and situation was further worsened by my deteriorating financial situation I encountered. Indeed, having money does not solve one's challenges, but having enough would greatly help one in addressing the problems one is facing. The real estate business was nationally and personally non-existent. I was having problems with my rental properties. The ones located faraway were even more problematic due to poor management and my poor health making it difficult to drive the 70 mile distance one way to check on the manager and the tenants. To pay my bills and feed my family, I was forced to dip into my savings. Unable to balance my books, I turned to my family for financial assistance. I will forever be grateful to my sister Fida Namususwa who frequently visited me at the company store and financially helped me. Fida also alerted my parents about the plight I was faced with. This may sound odd that I did not tell my parents, but I strongly believed that my mom and dad had helped me so many times that asking for any further help from them would not be in keeping with my personality emphasizing the need to be self-sufficient and not have the "entitlement mentality".

In keeping with this philosophy of self-help and false belief that with an MBA in hand, I dangerously started looking for other possible jobs that would pay me more than the meagre income I was getting from present company. I applied to many places, got many rejections, but naively believed that my inability to procure some of these great jobs was not because of the devastating effects MS was doing to my body, but rather because of the stiff job competition caused by the "2008 Great Recession." My belief in my strong qualifications became even strengthened when out of the blue I received a conditional acceptance offer from a recruiter agency wanting me to work as a loans officer in a bank. The terms of employment were as follows: there would be a

90 day probation period; the offer was in writing; the pay was higher than what I was getting. But health benefits would be effective after probation. There was no doubt that the overall package was attractive, not just because of the benefits, but also because this would be in keeping with my great desire to get a corporate job.

Before I was about to make the move to the bank, I had an epiphany that prevented me from moving away from my present company namely: I began working with a man at the company who was in a wheelchair. He would come into the store with a female friend who would help him get around to and from throughout the store and seemed to just watch over him, in general. On a close look, he looked familiar and so I made friends with him and started conversation with him. Specifically, this man resembled someone I knew from my high school days. I told him he resembled someone in a family I knew. I discovered in our conversation that this man not only knew the family, but he was a direct relative of that family. I also ventured to ask him what disease afflicted him so bad that he uses a wheel-chair. He told me that he had MS! That statement said volumes to me personally and I could discern immediately that his MS was probably not a 'viral infection', like I foolishly thought that mine was. I awkwardly replied to him, nonetheless, that I have also been diagnosed with the same. He offered encouragement to me since he understood the psychological effect of being diagnosed as an adult and dealing with the disease thereafter. To bring this close to home, he said he had the same type of MS that I had and he told me what medication he was taking. I suspected that his insurance must have been paying for his medication since the cost is astronomical! I could see from his muscle tone that he was probably confined to this wheelchair for some time. In my limited understanding, I wondered if this ailment was permanent or temporary for him and how this ailment has affected his career aspirations! I wondered if he was still working! Given that he came in on a wheelchair, how does he manage every day? But I could see that whatever the situation, the woman he was with was at the company store was probably there to help him manage this disease.

My decision to almost leave my present company and move to a bank was brought to a new light. Specifically, now that I could put a face to this disease, I began to understand that it was probably not a tricky "viral infection," but an ailment with devastating effects. I also immediately realized the importance of having an advocate or insurance or somebody to support you as you fight against this disease with the support of medication. I did not have an advocate about my sickness since I kept silent and I also realized that the 90 days wait without insurance could literally be life and death for me. With all this in mind, I declined the bank job.

My decision, subsequently, was to basically hold onto what I had at my present company, until I had my ailment had been brought under control. My limping and hobbling at all times, especially at the company made me guilty as my co-workers, could only guess what happened to me and why I was still working such a physically demanding job. But I knew that I needed my insurance to pay for my medication and other illnesses that may occur. Having weekly meetings, nonetheless, at this company painfully reminded me of my near demise on June 8th, 2008 and exacerbated my extensive PTSD. Without an advocate or even going to physical therapy, I thought that laughing and joking about everything and acting like all was okay was my best remedy to deal with all the pain. My pretense to my illness sometimes became so ludicrous that when I look back I do not understand what I was thinking! For example, I would get apologetic and even guilty when I would fall or explain to others why my walking and handwriting were impaired. Additionally, my daily sustenance and use of Copaxone as the medication treatment gave me the false hope that my current poor health was all temporary and in the end all would be well. Sadly, this pretense could not resolve my immediate problem of being literally financially destitute.

My parents knew that my income from my current employment was not enough to maintain my financial responsibilities. Due to my silence about my physical ailments with my MS, they thought it was just the economy that inhibited me from getting the job I went to school for. Generally speaking they knew what this recession was doing to many in the country, as well. Additionally, they knew that I was also having issues with my tenants in my rental properties, since some were not paying me rent after I fired the property manager for his financial improprieties. I did not have an instinct to evict these non-paying tenants like any landlord should. I was too fatigued and disoriented to drive to my home town to deal with the tenants. Additionally, I was experiencing major problems with the tenant who was leasing my other property. Rather than leave me deal with some of the self-inflicted problems and since I had ignored their advice they had earlier given me, my parents generously assisted me morally and financially. I hate to admit, but it is possible that without my parental assistance I would have sadly joined the class of people in this country referred to as "homeless." Their love, together with my readings from the Bible lessened the stress that I was experiencing.

To further lessen my stress, I decided to take a trip to the East Coast to attend my cousin's graduation. Such a trip, so I thought, would be therapeutic and it would give me a chance to meet with my extended family in general and Aunt Mangalita Dhadha in particular. Aunt Mangalita is special to our family because she was the first person my parents sponsored to come to the USA to study. She was inspirational in that she completed her requirements for her B.S and M.A from one of the state colleges. Auntie Mangalita also taught us a lot about Uganda culture in general and Busoga culture in particular. In other words, attending the graduation of Auntie Mangalita's daughter Fina was a major family event. What further made this strip significant was that it was not any party, but it was an event focusing on education – something which is greatly respected in my family. My parents strongly believe that education is the key to the development of any society. Consequently, my mom and dad have spent their scarce resources to sponsor many other relatives come to study in the USA. I also thought that the time of this trip in 2010 was timely as it would give me a chance to reflect on my life and enable me to make new career planning.

I was somewhat rejuvenated and optimistic that things would get better for me as this trip was approaching even though I was helplessly hobbling, tripping and falling. Fortunately, m employer gave me two weeks off from work so this abnormality wouldn't happen there as I reflected on m trip. But as I was finalizing the planning for everything for myself and the boys to go on this trip, 'Baby' decided that she did not want the boys to come with me. She had convinced herself that everyone in my family did not like her and she decided to show her disdain by denying the boys this opportunity. Her reasoning was ambiguous and unclear to me and like everything else with her, I did not allow myself to get bogged down with her random decision. I was, though, disappointed because it had been over three years since I took the kids to Ghana. Furthermore, I know they also wanted to get away like I did, especially since all their cousins would be there.

Regardless of these issues, I now knew that I would travel solo out east and so I finished getting prepared. A couple of days before I departed for my trip out east, much of my attention had been redirected to the World Cup soccer as the Ghana team had been getting a lot of attention internationally. Basically, they were beating opponents decisively and it just so happened that the U.S. team would be Ghana's opponent to get to the final eight in the World Cup. I am proud to be an American, but I now had children who can claim Ghana as their matrilineal roots while Uganda with me. Thus despite my love for the USA, I wanted the Ghanaian team to win and represent the African continent. I watched this game seated with my children and sister at TGIF restaurant in Bloomington next to the Mall of America. Everyone at this location were pacing to and from, but I remained calm in order not to cause a trip or fall. Although Ghana defeated the USA, their hope to get into the championship round was cut short by their loss to Uruguay because of an illegal handball that was caught on camera. The Ghanaians made an issue of the handball but eventually lost in penalty kicks. Although I was not happy they lost through penalty kicks, I was happy that they got their closure. But this reminded me of my situation with my work place accidents; but there was no closure with either.

In either case, I took a taxi to Minneapolis/St Paul International airport from where I flew to O'Hare airport in Chicago. Being in denial about my walking limitations and not to swallow my pride by succumbing to a wheel chair, I walked to the gate where my plane took off. This was an unwise decision because I profusely sweated and was disoriented as I stumbled and hobbled to my check in gate as I would stop and desperately hold on to the railings. Other passengers who were either walking with me or passed by me looked somewhat bewildered by my uncontrolled perspiring in an air-conditioned airport! After a long struggle, I made it to the gate and confusingly thought to myself that I had achieved something by walking such a long distance despite my ongoing poor health.

I soon forgot about my physical shut down at O'Hare airport and I relaxed and recuperated as we flew to our destination which was only 1 ½ hours in Pennsylvania. As I got close to my destination I had mixed feelings – there was the excitement of seeing my cousins, but then I became somewhat depressed because I was missing my boys and more importantly, they were going to miss the experience of reconnecting with their extended family. In keeping with my philosophy of internalizing personal challenges, I took a positive outlook based on the premise that getting away from my toxic social situation was a helpful thing in helping improve my health.

As soon as our plane landed and I stood up to get my luggage, my legs almost gave way under me reminding me of my ongoing elusive 'viral infection' type of MS I was battling with. I bewilderedly thought to myself that maybe this was because I forgot to stretch out enough following the torturous walk at O'Hare. I carefully walked off the plane balancing myself on the seats. Immediately afterwards I saw some of my family members from Minnesota like my parents, my sisters Olivia, and Monica with her kids. I also saw some of my family from the east when I exited the plane. Indeed, my spirit got rejuvenated within me when I communed with my family. All in all, I was happy to see everybody but I kept wondering why the boys did not come! After my difficult experience at O'Hare Airport, I was thinking about the distance I would have to walk to get to the vehicle that would take us to our place of stay. Fortunately, our vehicle was not that far away and the airport itself was easier for me to manage as it only had a few terminals.

As we drove to our destination, I immediately started to zone out of my families' conversation, oddly. I realized when we got to my auntie's house that I was extremely fatigued from all the activities leading up to our destination. They gave me some food to eat but I started to doze off as everyone was conversing. I reflected on the events of the day and I realized that all I did was sit on the two planes and watch the soccer game and walking around O'Hare in between, but why was I so fatigued? It was not necessary for me to stretch out just to stay awake, I thought. I did not juice, but I had a healthy breakfast and lunch with fruits, like Montel Williams with MS does and so my 'viral infection' MS should not be bothering me like this, I thought. Maybe it was because I missed my daily exercise? Nonetheless, it was daytime, and I desperately wanted to just take a solid nap, and so I did.

I rested s olidly while in a deep sleep and very comfortably for maybe 3 ½ to 4 hours. When I woke up and my senses fully came back to me, I realized that I had not rested so peacefully in a long time. I was used to sleeping with one eye open at my residence as I did not trust the surroundings around me. Nonetheless, my body felt much more relaxed than it usually did. But I thought it was because I ate healthier on this day with the fruits and all. That probably was partially true. But, I wanted to go for a walk or play basketball but instead I stepped aside and did some push-ups privately. I wanted to move around some like running or walking, but since I was not familiar with this area and I was not sure if my 'viral infection' MS would act up I stayed situated. Regardless of this activity, I had difficulty balancing myself with these simple push-ups, as well. My right side was weaker and it did not feel as strong as my left. This had become more apparent to me recently, but it was very significant today. However this was the opposite of what I expected since I was so rested and so I thought I was not doing something correctly with my push-up technique. Because of this slowdown, nonetheless, the rest of my push-ups were done with a grimace.

My legs were still nagging from my 'viral infection' type of MS, however, and so I did not add to my exercise by doing jumping jacks because I did not want to fall over and bring negative attention to me. But I noticed that even though it was comfortably warm outside, I was sweeting immensely from this exercise. After my exercising, I just sat down and cooled off. I looked around and no one was paying much attention to my futile attempt to exercise but my sister Monica. She looked at me like she knew that something was bothering me; but I just smiled and kept quiet. Indeed, exercise is very good. But, none of the exercises I did had anything to do with the MS I was diagnosed with.

Within hours nonetheless, my entire family on the east coast was at my auntie's house, including my younger cousins, who were also coming in from different states out east. The younger kids were inquisitively looking for my boys as that is where the good times were. I was saddened as I would tell them that they were not with me. It bothered me to say or even think about this because it was summertime and the reason for them not being there did not make sense to me. I observed that most of my other young cousins from just a few years back at my wedding in 2004 were now grown up and moving ahead with their lives in pursuit of a career. Indeed, my cousins were positioning themselves for successful careers in the future. Their dreams and aspirations were becoming more of a reality as they all were studying and working hard. Furthermore, my uncles and aunties were also moving ahead with their professions. It was obvious moreover that my family had a contagious and overcoming drive that was showing itself with everyone.

The question that kept lingering in my mind as I interacted with my family was why is it that despite having two degrees, which are a BA and an MBA, my professional career appeared to be stagnant? My personal answer to this was the view that the adverse effect of the economic recession which hit many people in the USA, but in particular those who were in the real-estate sector must be the culprit. Indeed, I realized my health was compromised because of my 'viral' type MS, but I foolishly thought that I was not the only one with such a challenge. In other words, I could still aim to achieve my professional career objective my poor health notwithstanding. Besides, I argued to myself, that despite the great benefits I was getting from my current employer, I could still get the same benefits (including health insurance) at other jobs. The bottom line was that I was confusingly not at peace with myself working a retail job, despite my excellent academic qualifications and the work experience I had!

This vacation stay was limited as it was only for a weekend. Subsequently one cool evening before we were scheduled to depart, everyone went for a walk outside to get some exercise and enjoy the beautiful scenery in the neighborhood. I had already made some friends down the road that moved in whom I met and I wanted to talk to some more. Instinctually therefore I was determined to go for this walk until I stood up and started moving around in the house. I had second thoughts when I immediately discovered how sore and weak my bones were when I almost tripped and fell as I attempted to walk to the restroom. Even though I had been seated and relaxed for several hours, I concluded that this was my 'viral infection' MS acting up and so I declined to go for the walk. But my denial perverted my senses and was now such a common occurrence that I refused to let myself accept that this was actually the MS prognosis coming to pass in my life.

After the day ended, we had our evening cup of tea, watched some more of the world cup of soccer and conversed. Our conversations were educated and about random topics. One such topic that came up in our conversation was about medical doctors and how they will relegate diagnoses for something they do not know as just 'viral infections'. Everyone seemed to have experienced this oddity, but there was no harm because everyone recovered and was healthy and on their respective paths to success. Notwithstanding this fact, I thought this was unusual for me with my 'viral infection' type MS that would not seem to go away but seemed to inhibit me daily. Nonetheless, I awkwardly laughed and smiled with everyone and drank my tea. I was not settled as something just did not seem right with this commentary considering the traumatic health woes in my recent past, which I could not think too clearly about. Strangely, I did not speak to anyone about it and how those 'viral infections' almost put me six feet in the ground when I was dying of a food allergy. I kept my silence and just excused myself from this talk and thought to myself about 'viral infection' talk we just had. This talk was complicated for me as my PTSD from February of 2003 ailed me severally while my current health was rapidly declining because of my MS diagnoses on June 08, 2008. I had a lot of loving and intelligent family members, but I did not know how to ask for any help in dealing with those 'viral infections' type of celiac and MS diagnoses. I just kept quiet while I was seated.

I rested very comfortably that night, before my departure the next morning. I was excited that everyone was doing well and competitively looking to make a name for themselves in their professions. I vowed to do what was necessary to better my professional career, despite the challenges I was facing. I must, though, admit that I foolishly comforted myself that nobody sees that there was anything wrong with me. What complicated my situation is that I had neither an advocate in the form of an attorney nor did I have a confidant who would have helped me understand the reality of the situation. Regardless of the circumstances I had to return to Minnesota to face my toxic social condition, but happily reuniting with my boys was my encouragement.

The return trip from the East Coast was not as problematic for me as the walking was not as extensive because I calculated how I would get around O'Hare in Chicago. To keep my sanity when I got home, I kept my faith by studying the scriptures and going to Church with my boys. In fact, it was around this time, I finished another iteration of reading the Bible but I was cautiously excited for what was next in my life. I say cautiously because I was a sick man and only getting sicker; but I had dreams and hope for the next chapter in my life thinking this 'viral infection' MS wouldn't inhibit them. My faith and personal confidence in scriptures additionally was exceedingly strong as my dream of understanding scriptures from years before was now becoming a reality. No one could take this away from me as I felt a personal connection with the Book itself. I would minimize my need to move around too much, and so therefore, nobody told me how badly my health was spiraling out of control. I loved to celebrate at Church because of my new found joy but I was in desperate need of medical attention and a personal or legal advocate. Notwithstanding this fact since I was in deep denial coupled with my mounting PTSD, I accepted all the pain and discomfort in my body as a spiritual attack from the enemy. I would therefore pray about it. But I desperately needed an advocate to help me realize and deal with the fact that this attack technically started in February of 2003 when I was indulging in eating forbidden foods.

Notwithstanding these facts, people would still see me hobbling around I believe not knowing the whole story. Besides my limping and imbalance, no one knew about the gravity of my issues and what kind of problems were going on with my physical and psychological health. MS was becoming ailment among all demographics of people, which I thought would help with my situation. But I thought that I did not look like someone with MS because I was on my feet and walking, albeit very carefully as I would evaluate the environment and where I would catch myself if/when I would slip and fall. But at the end of the day, I did not want to deal with this ailment by myself and I needed someone who could understand what was ailing me. Thus, in an attempt to open up to others, I would reservedly mention to some at my Church that I had MS, including nurses. But I do not think many knew what this was doing to me and my physical and psychological health. Perhaps this was because I just kept quiet regarding the details. Many of these people also saw me running around a gym recently playing basketball with other Church members. At that time, they did not know how much pain and discomfort I was in then. But at this point nonetheless, I was putting myself further and further into a ditch because of my silence at the same time, specifically with the time that elapsed from the accident. Thus my ailment was getting highly complex for me and others since my denial and disbelief was getting deeper. I also desperately wanted the ministry and fellowship at Church to understand what was going on since that was therapeutic to me as well. But this ministering was a temporary get away for me as my body was quickly debilitating from my 'viral infection' type of MS. At the end of the day, therefore, I still was not dealing with my problems I had in front of me which were quickly degrading my health as well as my psychological well-being.

Aside from my health woes, I was confronted with a depressing financial situation since my income had taken such a substantial hit. Indeed, I was working full time, but since the company had stopped giving any increases, my income was stagnant. I had all but given up trying to keep my rental properties afloat. But due to lack of funds and low energy which did allow me to drive to various places this quickly turned to be in vain. Thus, dealing with empty vacancies in my rental properties and collecting on non-paying tenants was not my priority. I accepted my fate as part of the overall sinking ship that carried victims of the nation-wide great recession. But just as I was struggling with these challenges, I received a job invitation interview with another company. I interviewed and was offered a conditional offer to work for this company. My spirit was rejuvenated in me since the pay was higher than my previous job and other benefits were just as comparable. I followed the protocol by meeting with my manager and explained to him what was going on. He wished me well and I foolishly resigned from my previous job in April 2011.

CHAPTER 6

A Plunge into the Unknown World: 2011 – Working at Several Companies; Continuing Social Challenges; Economic Hardships; Living with MS

When I resigned my previous position, I naively hoped I was going to have another shot working in corporate America. As it turned out, after 2011 I plunged into the world of the unknown dictated by the adverse effects of MS on practically every aspect of my life. What further complicated my situation was my continued denial that having MS was the center piece of my inability to get upward mobility in my career. Looking back in retrospective, I would have perhaps been better advised if confided into a friend about my problems I was facing. Lacking legal advice or having a confidant made me unwisely resign my position at The telecommunications office without carefully reviewing what could happen.

The first example of the negative effects of MS on my career were manifested when I interviewed for a position at the prospective company. My lack of advice and economic desperation I was experiencing failed me to realize the warning signs when I went for the interview at this company. The day of the interview, I put on my best suit, being helped by my son who helped me button my shirt since I had lost my coordination. As I excitingly proceeded to limb into the building to check in for the interview, my right food suddenly caught on a floor mat on the ground. With no time to react and nowhere to lean myself on, I wiped out and fell on the ground.

Everyone immediately stopped and stared at me. There was an awkward silence and bewildered stares. Straightaway I picked myself up turned around and embarrassingly looked at the ground like I did not see the floor in front of me? I had not even started my interview, but now I had to explain why I just fell on my face. After a few minutes, the silence ended and business continued. It was time for me to meet the interviewer who called me into her office. She was an energetic, youthful and attractive woman, who I later discovered was a former cheerleader for the Minnesota Vikings. She was not a salesperson for the company but was like a secretary just recording if I was present. I thought the first question she would ask me was going to be about my trip in the hallway or if I was okay, but she just smiled and took my name. Basically, she acted like nothing happened and so I therefore did the same. She then looked like she was impressed with how I was dressed and my resume. I smiled a lot during the interview, but I thought my 'viral infection' MS was too much of a distraction with my trip and fall. She asked me some general questions and said they would be in contact with me. She did not act like the boss I would be reporting to, but more like a gatekeeper. She instead just filed my resume aside and so we stood up and shook hands since she had several other people she was interviewing. I therefore turned around and proceeded to limp out of her office as I could feel her watching.

Since nothing was said to me with about my obvious physical irregularities, I convinced myself that all was fine as my PTSD kept me in denial with what transpired on June 8th, 2008. As I drove a way, I thought what was in front of me was bright. I felt like I accomplished something after my interview and I accepted what happened in my past as just history. I was encouraged as I was energetically greeted by my boys. They immediately wanted me to take them to the park and waterpark. But as I was getting ready to go to the park, I had several problems to deal with unbuttoning my shirt like I did with the buttoning.

Soon after I arrived at the park, I felt extremely fatigued and tired. This was more than usual and so I foolishly reasoned to myself and I thought it was because I was so excited for this interview which could help me move ahead with my career aspirations. I did not want to get out of my car and so I took a nap. After I rested for about one full hour, I had to use the restroom which was a good 200 yards distance from where I was parked. I got out of my vehicle and started walking towards the restroom. Straightaway, my legs felt like they were going to give away from under me and my bones were sore. I once again foolhardily thought it possibly was because I did not eat the right foods or I ate too much of the wrong substance! Maybe I needed to stretch out more, I wondered? Or maybe it was because I had not worked out? As I confusingly thought about these matters as I was walking to the restroom, my right leg began to drag as I was pacing. Before I knew it, my foot began to drag as I was watching the softball game and wishing I could play. Before I knew it my foot caught on a crevice on the sidewalk and I fell face first onto the ground. This time around fortunately, I was able to fall onto the grass and lessen the gravity of my collapse by catching myself on a picnic table. Several people who saw my fall probably wondered what caused this accident. I got up and slowly and carefully finished my walk to the restroom paying attention to the ground in front of me. I eventually made it to and from but I soon forgot what had just transpired.

On my way back to my house, I reflected on the events that happened to me from the interview to taking the kids to the park. I realized I was mentally exhausted from all the drama with the tripping and falling and my bones and muscles were still sore, too. But I accepted my general fatigue as just part of my regular being at this point. I ignorantly thought this was a good day for me. I say this because I interviewed for a job that would move my career ahead and put me back on track with what I went to school for, I thought.

One afternoon as I was struggling to stand on my feet, I received a conditional offer from the company I interviewed with for a business to business sales position offer. I thought I made a bad impression on them when I tripped and fell over a rug at their office. But then again,

I confusingly thought that maybe they could see past that mishap as a random fall or they did not notice it with all of my limping. To further distort my reality, this offer explained that my earning would be unlimited in a sales capacity and that they would offer all kinds of benefits like I had before. The only caveat I had was a 30 days training period that I would have to complete before I would realize any of these perks. Without an advocate to tell me how wretched my health was because of the June 8th, 2008 fall. I foolishly thought this was my key back to financial prosperity.

Without an advocate, I began to absent mindedly reason the logistics of this offer to myself. I had enough medication for 1 month and I thought I would be able to sustain until my new insurance kicked in. I was barely caught up on my mortgage because my salary was not enough or equivalent to what I went to school for. But I thought that I would be back in smooth sailing after I collected some pay checks from my new career. My responsibilities to my rentals were gone at this point because of non-paying renters and vacancies. But even if I would have had them, my energy to manage was exhausted because my 'viral infection' MS greatly had slowed me down.

I further thought about these matters, I knew I needed to speak with my manager at my current company. Interestingly, he did not seem surprised when I told him that I received this job offer! Conversely, he was friendly and told me what I had to do in order to finalize matters as a former employee. I followed his instructions and amicably terminated my employment in April 2011. I also thought if this opportunity did not work, I could come back to my former company where I had friends and I was leaving on good terms. At the end of the day, finally, I shortsightedly replied to this offer with an adamant yes! I was done at the previous company, I thought. I could finally put an end to this economical pitfall for me and get back on the big money route that I went to school for. I abruptly made this move without a legal or personal advocate. I had a family to provide for and I was drowning in personal debt with only my present income and with no hopes of advancement there I needed to boost my total income, I reasoned to myself.

I thus left the previous company limping and short of my cognitive abilities because of my injury there. But my decision to leave this company with the June 8th, 2008 mishap and an MS diagnoses at work was a highly dangerous and perhaps the most ill-advised move I had made to date in my life. I say this because at this point I would live with this debilitating disease without any insurance or ability to buy it on the open market because I had a pre-existing condition, if need be. Things happened so quickly and I thought I had this under control. Without an advocate, this was another bold and foolish step I took down an ominous road. For the record, I could barely walk, my writing was compromised and I was always fatigued at this point. I kept quiet, but the physical signs were more apparent.

Notwithstanding my PTSD induced silence, I thought I was ready for some business to business sales where I would be on my feet all day! I was ready to move on with my career. I would have to start with their training classes where I would be sitting behind a desk all day. These classes and all business there started early and 7am is when we would start and so 5am was when I would have to start. I knew dress was formal and professional and so I had my clothes put aside. I thought it was good because I was used to waking up early as I liked to study my Bible early in the mornings. I was excited to start my new career when the morning began. I therefore studied my Bible and I began to get ready. But my hands froze up on me when I began to button my shirt and straightening my tie was a hindrance too. At first, I thought it was because I did not eat the right foods for breakfast, but time was not on my side to figure it out. I kept trying, but I did not look right without my shirt buttoned right. I eventually woke up my eldest son and asked for his help. He helped me button my shirt and I quickly tied my tie and got out the door.

I smiled and tried to look cool when I got to their office as I passed by people in the parking lot. But in actuality I was very anxious, tired and stressed out. It was my 1st day and I wanted to make a good impression. Therefore I watched the ground as I walked up to the office so I did not trip over anything. I felt that my 'viral infection' MS was acting up as my right leg began to drag as I was walking. I did not want to trip on the steps once I got in the building and so I therefore took the elevator. I had 15 minutes before we began work. After introductions, the sales manager was brought in and we had a chance to briefly converse. He just had come back from Atlanta from a conference and based on how he was dressed, I could see he was making a very good income. I immediately could see myself getting paid like him, but I knew I needed to shake off my 'viral infection' MS first.

The first day continued with sitting down, taking notes and examinations. I enjoyed sitting down as opposed to constant movement because I thought this was good for my 'viral infection' MS. But I was extremely fatigued throughout the day. Additionally, I was not at liberty to get up and use the restroom on an impromptu manner as breaks were limited to one an hour. When our break time would arrive and I did stand up I would rudely discover straightaway that my bones were very sore and I could not even move, oftentimes. Walking around to and from was a major challenge and I would have to be extra careful not to trip and fall.

Finally, at 6pm we were dismissed after our crash course into the business. Even though I was seated the whole day, I was extremely tired. My body was also sore like I had just finished a rigorous work out. Since I knew I had not done anything but sit down, I started to think what I would to do to exercise as I drove home. When I got home my boys asked me to take them to the park. It was fair outside, but I sat down on my sofa and I suddenly could not move my body. I just shut my eyes and slept. Personally I was not happy with how I felt so fatigued and I had not done anything physically demanding! But I just figured I need to watch closer what I eat to pacify my 'viral infection' MS and also get more sleep to prepare myself for the rest of the week. I knew exercise was important still, so I managed to use the elliptical machine for 30 minutes with soreness and stiffness lingering in my bones.

In the interim I was looking to complete day two of my training. But when I woke up the next morning, I was helplessly exhausted with sore muscles as I could barely move and I had to get ready for another demanding day. I could not figure it out as my work out was not strenuous from the night before. I started the day by reading my Bible and praying that God would take away the nagging pain I had. I also did some stretching out as a 'doctor' who kept diagnosing with viruses once suggested as I had the same issues when I consulted with him; but the nagging continued. I ate a well-rounded breakfast with fruits since that helped others from what I saw on TV; but the nagging persisted. As was common at this point since June 8th, 2008, I struggled to button my shirt as I got ready so I asked my son for help. Unlike other mornings, I was extremely fatigued at this juncture and I just wanted to go back to bed. I did not want coffee or another stimulant to get me started, and all I wanted was to rest. I was not looking forward to another 9+ hour day and I was not sure how I could lessen the agony of this 'viral infection' part of my MS.

Regardless of my thoughts, I had to hurry up and get out of the door. I did not want to walk too fast or even run because I did not want to trip and fall. When I got to the company parking lot, I strategized where I would catch myself if I tripped or lost my balance. I could not afford to mess up my suit and bring attention to myself. I carefully watched the ground as I walked into the office and I smiled as I passed by people. I was very attentive once I got into the building because I did not want my foot to get caught on anything miscellaneous. At the end of the day, I did it! I managed to make it into the office without tripping. My next challenge was my cup of coffee which I carefully poured as I sat down. I was ready to begin the day.

My nerves were on edge as I sat down and reflected on the struggle to just get there. I was hoping that this day's activities would end sooner than 6pm like the day before as I anxiously waited for the trainer to start the activities. I was also hoping that my 'viral infection' MS would not act up uncontrollably as I stretched out and ate well beforehand. In the interim, everything began promptly at 8am but my mind immediately went into rest mode. Basically, I was mentally exhausted from the problems I encountered with buttoning my shirt earlier in the morning in addition to planning my walk and staring at the ground as I walked to the building so I would not trip. I tried to look up at the same time to make sure I was smiling, but subconsciously I was also fighting the depression with my PTSD. I looked good still and I do not think anyone caught on to my personal distress as I was painfully smiling. Like almost everyone else at this point, no one knew about the recent traumatic event that occurred to me on June 8th, 2008 or my PTSD associated with it which began in February of 2003. I did not know how to deal with these calamities but to personalize them and keep quiet. The cameras at both companies gave all the graphic and intrinsic details to qualify my behavior at this point. I also had adequate recourse with both situations as I was fully insured with both companies at the time of the incidents. But I did not plan for all the PTSD associated with them. Coupled with my silence, I did not know at this point how to ask for help because things were getting more and more complex as time went by. Perhaps most importantly, I did not have a personal or legal advocate so they could not plead my cause either.

I thought my silence had been working for me all along as I uncomfortably stood at breaks even though my bones and muscles were sore when I stood up for intercessions during this training. Nonetheless, I was looking to conclude day two as I came back to the reality of my present situation with training for my new job. My mind and body, nonetheless, were still unsettled as I randomly reflected to myself on events in my life. Notwithstanding this fact, the trainer said that on day 3 we would make some 'calls' to business to get in the field training. At first, I was foolishly comforted as I thought she was talking about making telephone calls and I knew that I could do that. But I soon realized that she meant to physically walk around and solici telecommunications products. My mind was not there in the training for most of the 2nd day of training. But I foolishly and optimistically thought the walking around would help my 'viral infection' kind of MS.

I was utterly exhausted by the time I got home. My boys excitingly greeted me when I arrived at the house. They asked me if we could go to the park straightaway, but I was utterly exhausted from just sitting down all day in training and all I wanted to do was rest. I felt guilty because the weather was nice outside and being at the park would have been therapeutic for me. The kids were disappointed, but at this point, I confusingly convinced myself that it was just my body reacting to the strenuousness of a full day with my 'viral infection' kind of MS. I thus put my head down and rested. Even though I ate and slept well I was very tired. At the end of the day, I ignorantly thought I was on my way to accomplishing something at my new job.

I woke up at 5am after about 10 hours of sleep and I got ready for day three of training. After studying my Bible and praying, eating a well-rounded breakfast and stretching out, I struggled to button my shirt again. I got out the door and walked with my head down so I would not trip over anything randomly and mess up my suit. Unknowingly my foot was dragging as I kept my eyes focused on my surroundings and I saw where I could catch myself on. This picture of me dressed up in a suit and limping around with my head down, I believe, was all an image of the downward spiral in my life since June 8th, 2008. But I convinced myself at this point that I was going somewhere with my life even though the MS had full control of my body.

No one at the new company knew what was ailing me as day three of training began. I therefore thought that no one could see my limping, dragging of my foot or grimaces when I was walking. The trainer began by going over what we would do that day and gave us some tips of the trade. We proceeded thereafter to get business cards and then they let us go out into the field. She did stipulate to us before we left by telling us to gather 20 business cards from different companies. She also mentioned that some companies may not be receptive to us and could make us leave by force. Lastly, we were given a zip code to stay within and then she dismissed us and told us when to come back to the office. Her advice that we may be forced to leave a company did not bother me at first because I was in good physical condition, I foolishly thought. Her directive for us to also get the cards did not seem too stringent to me as I already had dozens of cards from previous contacts and I ignorantly thought it would not be difficult to get more.

I drove off and proceeded on that note to get within my boundaries. I then stopped at a business and got out of my car. I was looking good and my adrenaline was flowing as I remembered the rush of looking for a sale in my mortgage and real estate days. But, my legs froze up on me when I exited my vehicle and I looked around to evaluate my surroundings and to see who was watching. I did a small stretch and started to walk towards the front door. I was used to walking with my head down at this point so I could evaluate the ground to avoid a sudden fall. Then it occurred to me that I needed to keep my head up, smile and maintain eye contact as that showed confidence. Also, I needed to see where my escape would be if I was met with hostility. Regardless of these facts, I painfully limped into the building trying to keep my head up and smile. I was met by the secretary at the front desk as I approached. I immediately looked for a place to lean on and catch my balance. I realized that I also had started to perspire. I think the receptionist could detect that something was wrong. Notwithstanding this fact, I introduced myself and I went through with the sales spiel. The secretary was hospitable and listened and gave me their business card. I then turned around and carefully walked away with my foot dragging and with my head down back to my car.

I sighed as I sat down in my truck and strategized for my next business. But I realized I had only one card and needed 19 more to collect in just 2 hours and yet I was tired and I wanted to just rest as I sat in my vehicle. I contemplated closing my eyes and taking a quick thirty minutes' nap, but then I realized that that could easily turn into an hour or more and I needed cards. Notwithstanding my fatigue, I pushed myself to move on and I drove down the road to the next business. There was a suite with several business inside and I did not hesitate to make my move on it. I realized that I could get at least 10 cards at these businesses unless I was kicked out. I parked as close to the building and then hobbled in. There were two floors and so I entered the first limping. I was sweating and I wanted to sit down. I noticed the first company's business cards were organized and on the counter. Straightaway I took a few cards and quickly introduced myself to secretary gave her my card and hobbled away. I hobbled and unknowingly dragged my right foot as I exited. After I painfully did the same at two more companies, I slowed down. My legs stopped moving! I needed to sit down or even lie down and rest. But the clock was moving and I had to get back to the office in 45 minutes! I panicked because they wanted proof, with the 20 business cards, and I only had 3. I decided to turn around and go back to my vehicle. I thought I was going to collapse as I tried to make my way down the hallway. I started thinking about shortcuts I could make to show my cards, if I needed to. I then realized that I had many business cards from this area as I used to do business with some of them in my real estate days and I could collect a few more on the way back. Thus, I made two stops on the way home and one was at a local Ghanaian shop named Agape. I knew the owners as I had done business with them a few years earlier while I was originating mortgages. It had only been a few years since they saw me shaking and baking to get a deal done for them, but this time around I was struggling to stand up and move around. Even though I was smiling as usual, I think they may have suspected something was wrong with me. I briefly communed with them but I had to leave. I hobbled my way out the door.

I tried to rush as I limped and dragged my foot unknowingly to get back to the office, but I was utterly exhausted. In no way was I looking forward to four more hours of training. I also was feeling uneasy because I did not have the 20 cards collected that the trainer said we should bring back. But I had other cards from previous contacts that I could present to her and I could follow up with, if need be, I thought. My reasoning, cognitive functioning and motor skills were noticeably deficient here as I soon forgot about all the pain and discomfort I was in because of my ailment. Nonetheless I thought I dodged a bullet, so to speak, as I could give those cards to meet my quota.

My body was at unrest as I got back to the company, but I managed to limp and hobble back into the office. I had a few minutes before our start. We got into conversation with a group I was training with as everyone already had stories about what happened to them when they went to different companies. Many people already had testimonies of getting kicked out of business and some of the stories were violent. But all I was shamefully thinking about was this 'viral infection' type of MS that was slowing me down. I also foolishly thought that maybe these receptionists and secretaries liked me as I was polite and looked professional. In actuality, they probably pitied me as I looked like I was going to fall over and pass out.

The trainer along with the manager were with us as we settled in after our 1st business selling run. They knew what everyone was talking about with the resistance at different businesses as they probably had experienced it too as sales people. I conspicuously kept quiet. Without any prior experience, I suspiciously looked cool like I had experienced that type of resistance before. I noticed at this point that some of the trainees had already. But my body hurt and I was exhausted as I kept painfully smiling throughout. Basically, I was living in a fool's paradise as I got sicker and sicker at this point and my running with the wolves in this business sales job was becoming a kamikaze endeavor. I say this because I was either going to pass out trying to do this kind of work or seriously hurt myself or somebody else. Unfortunately, my health insurance at the previous job was running out. At this point in time, I thought I could go back and work at my last job if this gig did not work out. I listened and let my body recover as the afternoon wound down and the trainer announced that we would be making more calls to business the following day. I think she could sense my discomfort as I shrugged my shoulders when I heard her statement.

We were dismissed and like the prior days, I wanted to lie down and rest. I had mixed emotions about what was going on with me as I drove home. Another nine hour day at work and I wondered if this type of 'viral infection' MS was going to subside. I ate healthy foods and I was getting proper rest and stretching a lot, but my body just hurt. The more I thought about what was making pains and aches so constant, the more I thought I was making it up and it was all in my head. To complicate matters nobody said or was saying anything to me about my obvious physical ailment. By the time I got home, all I could think about was day four of training. As usual, I was utterly exhausted but my boys rejuvenated me with their energy. I went to the gym with my boys at child care and had a mild work out with my 'viral infection' type of MS ailing me. After exercising, I needed a rest after day four of my training but I thought this job would provide an escape for me from the challenges I was facing and so I immediately got the boys showered up, prayed and went to bed.

I was cold this night but I did not sleep peacefully. I say this because my fatigue was extreme as many thoughts raced through my mind. Also, my nerves were on edge because I did not know if "baby" would set into her usual emotional eruptions either with me or friends she constantly talked to over the phone. My body hurt from this day's rigor with my 'viral infection' type of MS. The more I rested on my bed, the more I realized that I did not want day four to be as long and demanding as the previous one if I could shake this 'viral infection' type of MS. In the back of my mind I knew it would be as my eyes got heavier and I cautiously rested.

My alarm immediately went off and seemed like the snooze button only postponed the inevitable as I painfully woke up. I wanted to call in sick and I was frantically thinking about how I could avoid the inevitable misery coming my way on this day. I woke up and studied my Bible and prayed for a miracle. I then ate a solid breakfast, stretched out and proceeded to put my suit on. My coordination, balance and ability to button my shirt were completely out of alignment. I needed to move quickly to get to work on time and so I walked up the stairs to wake up my son to help me button my shirt. I was tired after the brief walk up the steps and I desperately wanted to go back to bed.

I painstakingly drove off to day four of my work endeavor. As soon as I arrived at the parking lot, I evaluated the walk area and the ground in front of me to ensure that I would not trip and mess up my suit. I proceeded to walk with my head down to ensure I did not trip on anything. I was used to walking with my head down wherever I went, but this action was now becoming a reflection of my struggle with my 'viral infection' MS. I would look up and smile notwithstanding when I would hobble by someone as if I had everything under control. I kept optimistic as I would think about the promises made to me as a believer in the Bible. This reminded me that everything would be okay. But as I approached the building and hobbled for my coffee and dropped down into my chair because of my imbalance, I knew only God could unravel the complexity of my situation.

The trainer proceeded to assign us area codes as day four began. She gave us some tips on how not to get kicked out of businesses. Finally, she said that we need to gather 100 cards and check back in at the office by days end! When I heard the card requirement, my heart sank deep into my throat. What was I doing to myself, I thought? Could I possibly gather 100 cards with this 'viral infection' type of MS before days end, I further pondered? Maybe they will have sympathy for my situation if I explain to them afterwards, I confusingly strategized to myself. Before dismissing us nonetheless, they put one of their more senior sales people to go with me until lunch time because she had work of her own to tend to. Others did not have this same type of help, I noticed. I think this was because they could see I was struggling to complete basic tasks, like getting coffee without spilling a little. Additionally, they probably could see that I was conspicuously quiet when everyone else had success and failure stories from days prior. Or maybe I didn't look well and they wanted to keep an eye on me!

What exactly was ailing me, they probably wondered. Besides falling on my face in their office when I first interviewed and the aforementioned oddities, they did not know what was wrong with me. This is because I had not said anything to them about this 'viral infection' type MS I had and how it was debilitating me, much like I had not told most everyone else either. My PTSD kept me quiet throughout because of my adversity from June 8th, 2008 and at this point this silence also perverted my judgment.

I started my 100 cards journey with a senior sales person to accompany me. We had a good discussion in the car and I could see that she was doing well in this gig. When we got to our area code, sales person in her came out which consisted of walking very, quickly from one business to the next while handing out her card and collecting theirs. I hobbled behind her as she got this done. But I realized from these activities that the company was basically looking for someone who could do the same as she was doing. Namely she was moving quickly and collecting several business cards.

I was getting more and more fatigued and I was looking for a place to sit down and rest. I think she noticed that I was tired, but like almost everyone else she did not know why. Regardless of this fact, she slowed down and asked me where I wanted to go to lunch. It was relatively early and I was not sure why she asked me this. Maybe she thought I was hungry because I was moving so sluggishly and with a limp? Regardless of her question, we had only collected 20+ cards and she knew that to hit 100, we would need to pick up the pace before lunch. But my body could not go any faster because my 'viral infection' type MS was having its way on my body. I was also profusely sweating as my muscle coordination was all but gone and I felt like I was going to pass out. But I pressed on limping and hobbling and every business I went into, I think, could most probably detect that something was grossly wrong.

Finally it was lunch time. I immediately realized that I had almost 40 cards collected and it was an accomplishment with my 'viral infection' type MS. I also needed to desperately rest my body as my vitals were shutting down and I was losing control of my body. Notwithstanding this fact, I also knew I would now need to collect 60 more cards for the afternoon. Honestly, the reason I was able to collect 40 cards thus far was because of the expediency of the sales person I was working with. I knew I was on my own after lunch because she had her own matters to tend to. I saw her moving quickly to and fro and I knew her example would need to be accelerated by me. The air conditioning in the building as I pondered on these matters helped me relax; but my whole body was still uptight. I stretched out before work and I ate my fruits for breakfast, but this 'viral infection' MS of mine did not let up.

After lunch and my body somewhat recovered and relaxed, we had to hurriedly get up and leave. We drove back to company headquarters and I got my truck. I knew I had to get back to my area code and so I painstakingly drove back to the destination. I arrived at a building complex with at least 6 different businesses. I thus got out of my vehicle, evaluated the ground so I would not miss anything that would cause me to fall and I hobbled into the building. I started to sweat by the time I got to the door and I was exhausted, but I went into the building and cooled off. I sat down on the furniture because my legs were uneasy as well from the brief walk from my vehicle that I just made.

After about five minutes of resting, I stood up and started my way to the 1st business. As I entered through the front door, I made eye contact with the receptionist. I could see that she was very, busy as the company probably was as well. I remembered how the sales person I was with would effortlessly gather cards, leave hers, and move on. I thought I could do the same. But I also knew that many sales people get thrown out too. With these factors on my mind, the receptionists looked stressed out and ready to explode as I approached the front desk. Regardless of this fact, I proceeded to limp into the office but my foot caught on the floor mat. Within an instant I was on my way to the ground; but I caught myself before I fell down. That was a very close call, I thought to myself as my blood pressure rose! I was sure the receptionist had other sales people approach her, but none with this kind of irregularity. Subsequently, she looked at me in amazement like what just happened? I did not know how to explain this 'viral infection' MS of mine, I thought. I just embarrassingly smiled, introduced myself, and gave her my business card and asked for hers. She confusingly gave me hers and looked at me surprised because nothing was on the floor but a mat that could have caused my stumble. There was a lot of awkward silence as we exchanged cards, but I just smiled, said thank you and evaluated the ground with my head down before my departure.

This was one down and now I had 60+ left as I made my way to the door. I was emotionally fatigued from that last stumble. I did not want to fall on the way out or have any other close encounters. I kept my head on the ground as I limped to the next business. I thought this act was to protect me from falling, but the reality that I was an ominous path became more evident. To help my walking, I was using the side railing or balanced on the wall as that brought me more security with each stride I made. By the time I approached the next business down the hallway, I wanted to sit down. I tried to act smooth and I smiled as I walked through the front door; but the pain and discomfort on my body, I think, were obvious. At first, this receptionists looked busy like the last lady, but she looked confused because she probably could see something was bothering me as I entered. Nonetheless, I introduced myself with a handshake. I leaned on the counter to alleviate some of the weight on legs and I gave her my card and took hers. Like the last woman she then watched in me in silence as I walked out. I carefully repeated this activity of mine for another five times and then I went to my car for a break. I rested for about 15 minutes. I then drove to another complex and carefully gathered five more cards.

I was moving at a slow pace that I only gathered another 15 by the 4:30. I desperately wanted to go home and take a nap. My entire body and legs hurt and I needed to rest. I confusingly thought they would not notice if I did not show up. I called a senior sales representative just to confirm, nonetheless. When I spoke with him, he adamantly insisted that I check in! No more, I thought. Is this a daily occurrence, I wondered? My days are almost 10 hours and this is not good for my 'viral infection' type of MS. I painstakingly wondered back to headquarters and I checked back in. I was exhausted and I looked beat up. My body was in pain as I arduously listened to the trainer. She gave us some parting advice and explained that on day five we will pick up the tempo. But I also had collected less than 40 cards and I was not looking forward to another day of pain and distress. Every trainee looked indifferent to her comment about 100+. But my disdain, I think, was noticeable. Therefore the sales manager pulled me aside and asked me if everything was okay. I had not said anything about my 'viral infection' type MS up to this point or talking about my experiences and I ignorantly thought he may be talking about something else. I also thought it would have been wrong to start now and so I foolishly said I was fine. Nonetheless he confirmed my productivity by looking at the number of cards I collected. After glancing at them, he solemnly looked at me as if to say something was grossly wrong and unacceptable because I did not meet the quota.

The writing was clearly on the wall for me with this career aspiration. But I still could not discern the inevitable! To insinuate the obvious, my manager's tone changed dramatically for the worse as he dismissed me. I think he figured that I would not come back for day five as the demands were going to increase as the trainer indicated. The only option for him if I did not resign or greatly increase my productivity was to fire me as I was not meeting expectations. Without an advocate, I ignorantly thought that the 'viral infection' MS of mine would magically subside. I therefore stood up and limped out of his office thinking I would be able to somehow run around and collect 100+ cards on the following day.

My drive home therefore was filed with confusion and fatigue. I could not explain these problems to anyone and the average person would not understand if I told them either. My body was aching and I was worn out. As I got out of my car, my boys ran to me screaming 'daddy, daddy!' I felt appreciated and I gave them hugs to show my appreciation. But they did not ask me to go play at the park and I was not sure why. I glanced at the babysitter to say hello as I grimaced walking up the stairs and I think she either talked them herself beforehand or just instructed them not to ask me because she was seeing my extreme daily fatigue. Indeed, part of what complicated my situation was that I just kept quiet about what was ailing me and I kept everything to myself.

I immediately passed out when I lied down on my bed. I was still in my suit but my senses just told me to rest. I heard "baby" come home and walk through the door soon after. I could vaguely hear her screaming on her phone and walk up the steps. She did not say much to the babysitter. Since she saw my vehicle in the garage and the kids playing in the back yard she may have thought there was something we were doing. Although I was 'sleeping' or resting with my eyes closed, I still knew what was going on around me and I watched her movements. I was used to this type of 'sleep' as I was usually on edge in case I would wake up randomly suffocating and out of breath.

She closed my door and let me rest and took the babysitter back to their home. I then began to rest and reflect on the day's events. I knew I miserably failed with my card collection at work. I could not keep up with the senior sales rep as she demonstrated how quickly someone in this line of work must operate. I absent mindedly could not understand why I could not keep up. But I knew I needed to change things the next day to make my productivity better. I embarrassingly recalled how I was hobbling, limping and nearly fell flat on my face when approaching a receptionist at a business. I once again foolishly thought that maybe that was because I did not get enough rest the night before. In actuality, I had had a 50+ hour work week already and my body and mind were not settled with this ailment. But I thought today could be different. Regardless of my confused thoughts, my body was utterly sore at this point as it had been all day, for that matter. I started to relax, I realized that all week it had been extremely sore and fatigued the more I thought about it. Foolishly I reasoned that this 'viral infection' MS just did not relax considering all the fruits I ate and stretching out that I did. Without an advocate speaking reality to me I ignorantly thought I could overcome health impediments the next day. I was getting more stressed out and fatigued as I thought about these matters in front of me.

I fell asleep until around 3am when I woke up. I was disoriented when I arose and I still had my suit on. I could not locate my boys at first until I checked their mom's room. Regardless of this matter, I was also sweating and my blood pressure was racing within me at this time. I was frantic this morning and I felt like I was living out a bad dream and the worst was yet to come. I prayed and went to my Bible to study and do my daily devotional. My heart was beating fast and my gut feeling was that this day bad things were going to happen to me. I proceeded to eat my breakfast which included lots of fruit; I then stretched out. My body was not getting any better and I felt that my time was running out with this 'viral infection' MS of mine. I confusingly personalized my ailment and I had all but forgotten about the travesty on June 8th of 2008. I blamed myself for my physical ailments. Maybe it was my diet and the nutrition I was not getting from my food or my exercise habits, I ignorantly thought. These thoughts intensified as I hobbled around my house looking for a railing or place to catch myself in case I tripped.

I had time this morning before my check in was required. Therefore, I watched the news and listened to some gospel music to get my mind off of my problems. I did not want day five to be as rigorous on my body as 3 & 4. I feared that I was going to pass out and the insurance did not start for almost 3 ½ weeks. I also knew that my medication would last for only 2 weeks. Like a lamb sent to the slaughter, I proceeded to move my way downstairs to get dressed. But my body was uptight and I was losing hope as all the fruits I ate and stretching out I did earlier did not seem to be doing anything. I continued with my fool's paradise that today I would get better. I still had plenty of time and so I matched the appropriate colors for a presentable suit and tie.

Finally, I was ready and got out the door. I initially had ample time to get ready, but now I was rushing because it took me so long to button my shirt and tie my tie. My drive therefore was uneasy as I was nervous that I would not make it on time. My thoughts of not wanting to walk too much fatigued me as this 'viral infection' MS of mine were running through my mind. My nerves once again intensified as I drove. I listened to some gospel music to relax. But each moment that I got closer to the headquarters the more the reality of intense walking endlessly became a reality. Besides my reservations and concerns, the drive was relatively smooth. I therefore made it to the parking lot with some time left before we began. As usual, I analyzed the ground to make sure that nothing would surprise me where I could fall. With my head down and balancing myself on the cars in front of me, I hobbled to the front door. I smiled as people went by me to make it look like I was in control.

I started to perspire as I entered the building. I was tired and my legs were sore. I could not bear the thought of having to do this all day. My body and mind were shutting down as I was anticipating the trainer to begin day five of our training. I had a few minutes and so I got my usual cup of coffee. Even though I had been awake since 3am I was not even craving coffee like I usually did. I was operating on nervous energy because I just knew that today something bad was going to happen to me since I did not want to walk around everywhere. I had cooled down, but I was still perspiring. I liked challenges but this nervous energy was like nothing I had ever experienced!

The trainer walked in promptly at 8am. She immediately assigned us to different area codes and told us to stop back at lunch. Straightaway, I noticed that there were other sales people who were making phone calls as we were dismissed. Therefore, I decided to do the same thing as the other trainees left for their card collecting out in the field as the trainer instructed. I was desperate and I thought no one would notice. I got on my phone with business contacts that I had previously come in contact with and I made some phone calls. But within 10 minutes the manager called and told me to come to his office. I ended my call and hobbled to his office. As soon as I stepped in to his office, I noticed that there was a woman seated next to him. I was instructed to sit down and the manager told me that I was not going to work at the company any ore since they have terminated my employment. I panicked and I told them that I had MS. I did not try to explain my 'viral infection' because I was not sure how to or even what it really was. They both looked shocked and the Human Resources woman looked sympathetic as she knew 1st hand how wickedly debilitating the disease is. But she replied after a moment of silence saying that I did not mention anything to them beforehand and therefore they treated me like everyone else. They were correct in spite of my tripping and hobbling. Even though my timing was poor, it was nice speaking to others about what was physically ailing me, I thought to myself. I proceeded to stand up evaluate the ground and know where I catch myself in case I tripped. I walked with my head down to confirm I was seeing everything correctly. I could feel them watching me as I hobbled out of the office.

My ominous path thus continued as I thought of what was next for me. The loss of this job involved the loss of income in general and the end of my expensive monthly insurance drug benefit the company was expected to pay so I could continue on my medication. I thought I did all this to myself by failing to report the workplace injury I had at The telecommunications office and because of my lack of proper nutrition and exercise. I blamed myself as I thought how everyone in my family had their health issues and even marital problems; but they were all able to overcome them and move on with their careers and lives. Why could I not do the same, I misguidedly thought to myself as I approached my vehicle?

As I drove home I reflected about how I managed to overcome the obstacles in front of me in everything I put mind to. I thought along these lines because I was not going to let my failure put my head down in shame even though I needed to hobble looking at the ground. I was highly confident that I could overcome any setback. This attitude was an overcoming attribute I got from my parents. Along with my siblings, we all exhibit this trait in our personal life experiences. To remind myself of my own plight, I briefly remembered my college days as I drove home. Specifically, I remembered how I overcame tremendous obstacles to prove to myself and others that I could just make it by graduating. I also remembered my plight in graduate school afterwards and how I was able to work full time and complete this degree. I then recalled how I purchased three houses at the same time to keep me and my family financially afloat amidst all of the obstacles. I knew God was with me for that matter, throughout the entirety of these events and then He graciously blessed me with my two boys on top of all that. But I had gone into isolation as I was thinking of these things. I knew God was guiding my footsteps and I thought I could do this again, if I put my mind to it and corrected my shortcomings I did that would heal all my health woes. I therefore foolishly thought I had all this to myself to get this 'viral infection' MS under control. Thus, although I was physically and mentally fatigued I convinced myself that I could still forge ahead and attain my career ambitions.

I knew what my limitations were with work and so I decided that I wanted to apply for jobs where my physical limitations due to this 'viral infection' MS would not be a factor. Indeed, I did not want to be on the sidelines for too long and so I limped and hobbled to the library to get my resume out there. I was fairly confident I would not be on the sidelines for long because I had the qualifications for every job I applied for. I applied to hundreds of jobs in the time I had this afternoon. Before I knew it about eight hours elapsed between the coffee shop and library after I was let go and so I decided to go home. My body was sore as usual and I was tired even though I was not walking everywhere like I was required to do at the previous job. I was expecting an e-mail or a phone call from a recruiter over the weekend or first thing Monday of the next week for my new career. I shared my confused excitement and joy with my parents along with the bad news of my layoff. Indeed, they were disappointed about what happened. But they were excited to hear that I rebounded in no time at all albeit with some reservations. They were uneasy that this company just let me go only after five days. But I was not clear with them as to just how strenuous this job was on my body. In fact, my body was on a rapid downward spiral but I was not telling them all the details about how I was feeling. They knew we were generally in a recession and so without all the information at hand I think they just relegated my employment woes to that. Our conversations usually were just me checking in and saying hello but nothing too much in depth or specific about anything. I came across relatively confident that something would come up straightaway. Since they had seen me hustle in the past to make things happen, they were not overly concerned. They knew how excited and determined I was to start this new career. But they also knew how vital the insurance was pivotal with my $6000 a month medication to handle my 'viral infection' type of MS. They still had not seen all the deterioration with my walking or general health. Many in my circle had not seen this deterioration unless they saw me walk around to and fro, like at The telecommunications office, or just long distances, in general.

Regardless of these facts and circumstances, I slept comfortably over the weekend after the pressure of that sales job was gone. That episode of my fool's paradise about getting another job straightaway came to an end on Monday morning. Basically, reality sounded loud when my alarm went off and I did not have a job to report to. I did not know what to do or where to go. I felt confused and abandoned. I could not understand what I did not have that these jobs were looking for. But I still went through my morning Monday through Friday routine as I limped to and from. At the end of the week, I still was not getting any responses from my job applications. I was also running out of my MS medication injections as I could count less than 10. Although I am good at networking, I still was not making headway. In spite of the frustration I was confronted with, I naively believed that with my good work record and decent public relationship, I could apply to get back to working at my telecommunications company. I therefore called my former manager and expressed my desire to want to come back. He invited me to lunch at Perkins where we could discuss matters. My parents took time off from their demanding schedules and escorted me to meet with him. At first, we laughed when we met at Perkins as if nothing had changed since my abrupt departure a week and a half earlier. But after I asked him if I could return to the company to work at his store, his demeanor changed. He immediately said that he would love to do that, but there were some write ups from years earlier that prevented him to allow me to go back. I froze up when he referenced that location and 'write-ups' as that is where I should have died on June 8th, 2008. I think if I would have mentioned anything to him about that day and the liability his company had incurred towards me, he would probably not have hesitated to accept me back.

At the end of the day, my thoughts went everywhere when my former manager said he was not looking to hire me back. First my heart temporarily sank into my mouth since I thought that my former manager was my friend! He knew that I knew all of the systems and I was a very good sales person. My pride would not let me show him or my parents how rejected I felt, however.

After telling me how the write ups inhibited his decision to hire me back, the former manager reached in his pocket and got a wad of cash and said he would pay for lunch. He then proceeded to tell me about his plight to get to where he was as a manager at the store. I was not sure what was going on as I confusingly shook hands with him to conclude our meeting. I was shell-shocked and overwhelmed that he referenced those frivolous write up incidents at the store without mentioning what happened to me on June 8th, 2008.

I proceeded to confusingly explain to my parents what my manager's reasoning was to not take me back. But they could not understand how I worked faithfully for them for almost three years and after only 1 week away they would not hire me back. They knew that we were still in the 'great recession' and so they attributed this woe of mine to that. I kept quiet as I knew that something more was grossly wrong with me and how my woes started on June 8th, 2008 when I was injured. But I silently and painfully accepted the 'great recession' as the cause of my problems and inability to hustle as I usually did as I confusingly stumbled away. I attributed none of my obvious medical problems to my diagnosed MS. Conversely, I foolishly and bewilderedly treated it like it was just another 'viral infection' because of previous questionable medical treatment.

Without dealing with my medical issues, I thought I would just have to continue hustling to find something else rapidly. I was therefore foolishly confident that I would rebound from my setbacks at the previous companies I worked for. I thought I needed to focus my attention on getting a job where I would not need to walk or even write much as that was also deteriorating rapidly. It therefore did not take me long to get online and start researching and applying to hundreds of jobs online.

Before I knew it, several weeks had gone by and I had not found a job. My medication also ran out and I had no insurance and I was not insurable at this point. I networked at the coffee shop, but that was unfruitful too. I started bringing my boys with me to the coffee shop and library to these activities. I brought them because I loved them and they brought me hope and encouragement that everything would be okay amidst the chaos.

I was in a precarious and highly complicated predicament without a job, uninsurable with tremendous and mounting PTSD. The month of June was winding down and all I could do was continue applying to jobs and networking. I knew I could not do most work I researched as I could barely walk or write or do any physical activity as my motor functionality was all but gone. I still pressed on nonetheless. But I soon realized that with all my efforts disqualifying jobs that would not work for me I only found jobs that were not straight forward or required only a high school education. At the end of the day, I felt like I applied to around 500 jobs all of which I was not making any headway! Maybe recruiters saw me as overqualified with my college degree or MBA, I confusingly wondered!

Regardless of these ill-advised thoughts of mine, my bills were simultaneously over taking me as I had no cash flow. One of those bills was my mortgage! My rental houses were all gone as 'the great recession' coupled with theft and mismanagement by the management company and my 'viral infection' type MS inhibited me from properly caring for them. Everyone knew what this recession was doing to many. With me, my mom therefore took the lead to organize the family to help out. To assist me, my mom invoked my family, who knew I was in distress and the general details of my plight, to step in to help me out. They also knew that I was 'sick' with MS type symptoms and perhaps something else. But with the information and medical metadata out there coupled with all the knowledge in my family I think they saw the MS as a hindrance more than a debilitating disease since this wasn't common with black people or our family. With that information aside, I was now a face, perhaps the 1st, in our family with this disease? As much as I appreciated the family assistance, I was at the same time embarrassed by the fact that I was putting financial stress on people's scarce resources to help me with my never-ending problems that seemed to have recently started from my work place injuries.

Due to this guilt, I continued to apply to jobs in my physically limited capacity where I would not need to walk or write much. As I disqualified myself from most type of work, I came across a help wanted for a company that I was familiar with. It was the same gold and silver company named BCC where I previously worked some years back. They indicated that people can earn unlimited income and I would not need to walk much. This was the same spiel that caught my attention years back. I therefore thought that this was my gateway and door into furthering my career aspirations. But my optimism was met with reservation as I remembered my previous experience at this place.

I had not heard back from the numerous jobs I applied to and so I moved ahead speedily regardless of my concerns. I contacted their office and I was told to come in and apply. I thought this was somewhat odd because I knew they still must have had my information from my 1st application a few years back. But I proceeded to go back to their office and submit another application. Unlike the 1st time, I struggled to walk into the office building and barely legibly completed the application. Although the receptionist could barely read my handwriting, she filed my application away like it was nothing major. She also was very formal with how she handled matters only calling people by their last names. To an outsider, which is what I was, the impression was that this was a fast moving shop where major trades and exchanges were done at stock market rapidity. Nobody gave me a straight forward answer with the benefits at this place, but I got the impression by the formality that everything was in place. To confirm for myself, I asked the receptionist if they had benefits and health insurance with this job. She immediately answered me by saying that I should check with the owner of the company.

I was then instructed to have a seat, which I desperately needed anyhow. There were a few of us at the office who showed up for the job posting but they were already seated. Within minutes, a middle-aged guy proceeded to walk towards us with booklets and he said that we needed to read the booklet and learn the facts on gold. I could detect straightaway that he was making good money. But as he started talking to us, two people walked by him who looked inebriated. They made no eye contact with any of us but were just laughing as they walked by. Regardless of this oddity, those guiding us never paid any attention. I was instructed to read the booklet I was given, that the dress was formal and that work starts on Monday. I was told that I would draw a small check each week which I would pay back once my commission came through. He told me I was the frontier and he would be the closer. The meeting concluded and I felt good to be back in the hustle, even though I thought this was odd and somewhat unprofessional.

In spite of all my observations with these people, I limped out of the office thinking that my career aspirations were now back on track. But the same unanswered logistical question I had when I went to one company instead of another years earlier were still the same questions I had at this point. Namely, I still did not know what benefits or insurance I would have. I tried not to think about these matters for too long, but decided that I would cross-check with the owner on Monday, as I was advised to do. I therefore continued in my fool's paradise as I drove home. I was confusingly thinking that I could get back on my $6000 a month medication after I spoke with the owner.

I did not have a personal or legal advocate at this time and I foolishly looked forward to starting my new job and speaking with the owner about my benefits. I made sure that I was ready to go on Monday morning by stretching out and eating my fruits. Everyone was dressed formally but I felt a spirit of lawlessness and rebellion everywhere. I was told where to sit and I happily sat down as my legs were on edge. There were four rows of desks with one person seated at the front, who was called the closer. There was a fairly nice office for the senior closer. I was given a list of names and paper to write down my notes. Indeed, I liked sitting as that was good for my 'viral infection' type of MS, but they wanted me to write a lot which was not good for my situation. Even though I had stopped taking my medication because of my lack of insurance at this point in time, I was not going to let my illegible handwriting be a hindrance.

I had read through the booklet which was handed to me earlier at orientation and so I thought I was ready for the challenges ahead of me. Each call was different, but I was reading from a script. It was monotonous, but I had a natural gift to smell a sale. When I came across something that felt like a potential sale, I would encounter interference from other coworkers. They did not seem to be aggressively calling like me, but they were just waiting for me to get a lead and then put their names on the final paper work. I discovered the turnover was very high at this place because of these types of oddities. There was subsequently a lot of idiosyncratic behavior that sometimes turned violent because of territory and leads. Vulgarities and fights happened often starting with management! I soon discovered that this was the culture and the norm in this type of work. Infrequently, the owner would stop in and many times was either loud or yelling at someone at the top of his voice. He was a hefty set man which made his tirades intimidating. But I knew I needed to talk to him, per my instructions from the receptionist about my benefits and health insurance. I therefore waited for an opportune time to ask him.

After about two weeks from my start date, I started to get comfortable with the protocol. At this time, I noticed that he came into the building and he was not screaming. Conversely, he was smiling and seemed happy. I thought that this would be the opportune time for me to ask him about the benefits of the job as I was instructed. He was about to start a meeting with his senior executives and I knew I would have to be direct and time was of the essence. I also knew I would get more direction since the managers were present. I therefore casually limped to his office, looked him in the eye and asked him about their health insurance and when it would start. The other people kept deathly quiet when I asked and looked at each other. But without hesitation in the presence of his managers standing by, he looked me in the eye and said the insurance would start after 90 days. I immediately felt relieved when he said that, but I was not sure why I had to personally ask him when his managers could have told me the same thing. I acknowledged that I understood him. I then carefully turned around and hobbled out of his office.

I continued transferring and putting in hot leads but none of my deals were closing. My handwriting was greatly compromised and illegible when I was taking notes on my phone calls and many people I worked with probably thought I was illiterate, incompetent or mentally handicapped. I knew I was neither. I thus became frustrated since I could not pay my bills on the minimum pay check I was getting before closing any deals. As I earlier noted, the assistance I got from my family and friends was greatly appreciated and helpful. However, I was uncomfortable to continue to depend on others for my long-range life objectives. What further complicated my situation at this company was that the management was not forth right in presenting their policies to employees. For example, I was frustrated that neither of my hot leads were closing and I was not getting any feedback on them or paid.

As we approached mid-September of 2011, I tried to keep a positive attitude as to what I might get from this company. My 90 days had expired and I was eligible for their insurance. What a joke, I thought to myself! How can the president promise me health insurance after 90 days and no one knew anything about it? My body was weak and I was tripping and falling frequently in the office. I would pick myself up amidst odd stares and people asking me what happened. I would act like it was just a mishap. All I wanted were answers about the promised insurance. I tried to speak to the owner about this, but since he was busy most of the time I raised the issue with some of the people I was working with. To my surprise, some of my co-workers did not understand what I was talking about and others did not care about any benefits as long as they were getting a check from the deals they initiated. Consequently, the poor management of this company resulted in a lot of turnovers. I naively thought that I could discuss my frustration with one of the managers, but his reaction to me was hostile in that he regarded my attitude as rebellious and questioning his authority and so he fired me.

With this job gone, I went back to applying elsewhere. I stopped paying all my bills because I had no income. Around this time, my family intensified their concern and support. A case in point was the God-sent help I got from my sister Monica. She stepped in and started to ask me questions about my MS and gather information about the medication I was taking. At first I did not know where she was going with all her questions, but I just provided her with answers she had for me. I knew that she was working 70+ hours a week and taking care of her children as a single mother and so I knew how valuable her time was. Before I knew it, Lydia notified me that I would be getting a dosage of my medication (CoPaxone). This was a huge relief for me and my family as this meant that I had something to use to control my MS.

This advocacy by Monica with my medicine allowed me to think rationally for myself and reflect. As I thought about things, I knew that I needed to file for unemployment to get compensated from last company while I was waiting for my next gig. As I continued applying for new jobs the state of Minnesota was gathering information regarding the facts that led to my termination. I gladly told the state what had transpired. The management in this company were, however, uncomfortable about the state inquiries about their company and so to avoid any further involvement with the state, I was invited to work for the company for a second time.

Despite the great assistance I was getting from my family in general and Monica and my parents in particular, I accepted the offer to work for this company again. I strongly felt that by being employed with a company as questionable as this one, my family and friends could realize how much I wanted to lessen my dependency on others. On arrival at the company, I realized that not that much had changed, but I tried to ignore the short comings in pursuit of financial gains. To my disappointment, all the hot deals I was previously working on were all gone and all closed with other people's names on them. This was the culture at this place and so I had to start from scratch. Within one week I had three hot deals all of which were closed by my new manager which obviously greatly benefited him from the financial benefits that came out of these deals. Indeed, I made some money, but the major problem with this company was the lack of consistency in their policies. Consequently, I found myself permanently broke.

To lessen my never ending financial woes, I filed for bankruptcy in 2010. I initially felt that I had done the right thing since all my debts, except those related to the vehicle and house were discharge. However, when I closely reviewed what had transpired, I was still confronted with major problems. The house needed serious repairs and I needed a steady cash flow. Therefore, I was on the horns of a continuing financial dilemma – either providing food for the family or investing into the house repairs. I also faced the problem of the mortgage being dangerously behind and thus opening up myself to foreclosure! All in all this was a clear indication to me that I could not meet my financial obligations based on the income I was getting at this job. In order to find time to connect up with potential new employers, I asked time off from the company.

One afternoon at the fitness club, I got a lead from a friend who advised me to speak with a recruiter of a temp agency who was hiring for a big reputable company. I contacted the recruiter straightaway and without hesitation they offered me a conditional position, involving the following: I had to show up every day and do what I was being told and benefits would be granted if I fulfilled the 90 day probationary conditions. He invited me to go to the headquarters to finalize the conditional offer.

This offer made me feel that my financial woes were finally ending. I was moving on adrenaline. However, I struggled to move around as I was getting dressed, buttoning my shirt and preparing to drive to their headquarters which is located about 15 miles away from my home. On arrival at their location, I saw four to five massive buildings. I was intimidated by the great distances I had to walk and the overwhelming size of the interior layout. The recruiter was paged and he politely introduced himself to me, nonetheless.

He expediently escorted me inside, showed me some places inside the building, introduced me to some key people in the business area I would be placed in, and then continued to walk quickly inside the building. My legs were giving way and so was my right arm as I balanced on the railings to avoid falling off. I was praying to myself that we would stop walking all together because I wanted to sit down and rest. Eventually, we stopped and then sat down! The recruiter explained to me the requirements and compensation for the job, wished me well, and told me I would start work in the next two weeks. Naturally, this offer gave me hope for stability and normality. On the contrary, my family in general and my sister Monica in particular had mixed feelings about taking this new job. Monica with whom I had interacted on several occasions was more conversant with my limitations in taking up this job.

In retrospective, Monica's judgement proved to be the correct one. Every morning, I had a lot of adrenaline going through my body as I went through my daily routine. After studying my Bible, I made sure I took my medication and ate my fruits and stretched extensively. I struggled to button my shirt, but I woke up early enough to complete it. I made my way to the corporate headquarters wobbling as I checked in. The recruiter met me with the other recruits and then we sat down. I was uncomfortable because I could feel my 'viral infection' type of MS starting to act up. They introduced us to executives we would be working with. After an hour, we were allowed to stand up and stretch out, after which we started a tour of the facilities. This was a big challenge for me since fatigue had set in, making it difficult to keep up with the fast speed people were moving at. So fast was the speed that I began to sweat, despite the building being air conditioned. We stopped at locations and instructions were given, but I was unable to keep up with everything.

After our introduction and tour of the facilities, we sat down again. At this point my mind, like my body, shut down. I tried to keep my cool but my palms were sweating and I was also perspiring. All of the walking around that building without knowing when we would sit down just shook me up. I cringed at the thought of having to continue walking like this. But I just smiled to give the impression that I had everything under control. Fortunately, we were seated for the rest of this day and our week of training, so I discovered, was over. My major hurdle, thereafter, became walking from the parking lot into the training quarters. I ignorantly thought I was going somewhere when I made it through the week hereafter.

My body was extremely uneasy and I was excessively tired and fatigued after the first week of training. Working out, stretching out and eating fruit was doing me little to no good subsequently as my body was always on empty. But I ignorantly thought I had accomplished something after completing this task. I struggled to keep up with the demands of meetings. I was confusingly punctual often as I would be sweating after walking to meetings' but I thought I would get the official offer. I kept to my routine week after week. But the more I continued to push myself the more I would be fatigued. I was also trying to eat healthy, but if I slipped up and ate foods that I should not have, my stomach would pain me and slow me down. This was my 'viral infection' celiac allergy acting up, I ignorantly thought to myself. But, like elsewhere, I was a hostage to the bathroom and I would therefore miss and show up late to meetings because of digestion problems with my food. Coupled with my limping, stumbling and tripping, I was bringing unfavorable attention to my plight at the corporation. Subsequently I got a call from the recruiter within weeks and they told me that major retailer was no longer interested in my services as a temporary.

Even though I wanted to make the cut at this company, I knew in the back of mind that this would probably come to an end. Specifically, I could barely walk around the building to meetings or write legibly and I was always fatigued because of the demands and my stomach ached nonstop. I think they perhaps did not want to see what would happen next as I was near collapse everyday. But I ignorantly reasoned to myself that this specific type job was too much for my tricky 'viral infection' type of MS. I thus continued living in my fool's paradise since I thought I would find a job more conducive to my elusive 'viral infection' type of MS.

Although I did not miss the pressures of the job with constant meetings or all the walking around the buildings, I immediately missed the steady checks I was receiving. Besides my vehicle, I knew I needed to pay for my mortgage. I thus went back to applying to jobs online. I also went back to the company where I was selling gold. My heart was not into that job any more but I only needed to feel like I was a part of something. Additionally, I had several bills that needed to be paid. Everyone at this point, especially my mom, knew how my ailment was slowing me down tremendously as I was looking for work. Their support therefore intensified.

Fortunately, sometime around late August 2011, I got a lead online in customer service department in another reputable company. I applied for the job in customer service online and I got it. I carefully read the job duties and I was confident that I could perform it. This was a relatively big organization and I knew that I could move up as long as I could control my 'viral infection' type of MS. My initial problem with their process was that I would have to print and fill out an application. I knew this might bring attention to my 'viral infection' type of MS because my handwriting was often illegible. Therefore, I printed out the application and fortunately met a young lady who helped me fill it out. I immediately faxed it to the company who within days sent me an official offer. Since the job involved largely sitting down and talking on the phone, I was confident I would handle it efficiently. However, after a close review of the offer, I found out that this job was not as great as I had initially assumed. First the job was part-time with minimal compensation! Additionally, the job being located 30 miles from where I lived meant that I would probably spend a great amount of the bit of scarce resources I still had on gasoline expenses.

Notwithstanding my concerns, the orientation began in two weeks and so I had to act quickly. The first thing I did is relay this information to my parents. They asked me about insurance benefits, straightaway. I told them it was not clear but they were a big corporation and so it had to be part of their eventual offer. I then told the gold selling company that I would be leaving in a few weeks. I kept a positive attitude there as I knew that I may need to return again if my new job did not pan out.

One afternoon in October 2011, as I was getting ready for my new work, someone rang the doorbell. This was unusual because nobody usually stopped by as the home was rarely presentable. This random man was standing at my door with some papers and conspicuously looking around. I opened the door and he immediately asked me if I was

Nekemiah Muzazibwa which I confirmed I was. He then handed me the papers in his hand and said you have been served and then turned around and walked away. Bewildered I immediately thought what this could mean. The bankruptcy was discharged and so I was not sure what to think. I read a little bit and realized that these were divorce papers. Although I was generally overjoyed that I finally was going to get rid of some of my social problems, I was at the same time concerned with the timing of this divorce process at the beginning of my meagre paying job. There was also the financial challenge of burdening my family since I was broke. i happily discovered that through the help of my sister Monica, I got an inexpensive and caring lawyer, who also was my paramedic by helping me continue the medical treatment I needed through my neurologist and was also helping me to procure an apartment as the writing on the wall in my life was very evident. As with my family, my gratitude for her work increased manifold by this intercession from Monica as the stress it was imposing on me was tremendous.

Despite all this assistance, I was by mid-September 2011 so stressed that I was practically a zombie at my new at current job. I would trip and fall as I was trying to keep up and make deadlines. I just kept a smile on my face and apologize for not seeing the ground. I had made several friends here which was therapeutic for me, however. But part of what kept me unnerved in addition to my ailment was the fact that no definitive answers were being provided for my health insurance. I was told that I needed to work full time to realize this benefit. I found out that as a new employee I would have to wait until after 90 days of employment to go full time. My sister Monica was against my pursuing full-time work, but instead she invited me to go to her office where I learned that she was filling an application on my behalf to get social security disability. I was both happy and impressed that despite her hectic schedule she could find time to help me.

In addition to the family support and love I got, the church was my other support system. Although earlier I was an active church goer, I decided in November 2011 to switch my church attendance to a different location. The new church had the same roots as the Bible

College that I attended in St. Paul, but the only difference was that unlike the previous one the new church was predominantly black or African-American. I was happily received by my new Church. My new pastor was appreciative of my accomplishments and he appointed me as a minister, straightaway. I was highly encouraged by this appointment. I explained to him that I was afflicted by MS, hence my limping. This way, I felt people in the church would not ask me too many questions about my physical condition. The new church brought a lot of hope for me both spiritually and health-wise. I met several people who encouraged me to try all kinds of treatment.

In the midst of my continued troubles in 2011, I received the good news from my brother, Joshua Magezi and his girlfriend had delivered a healthy baby girl named Julia Edisa Mpayenda. I was overjoyed because I had been advising Joshua and his girlfriend, but also because they named their child after my mom's maiden name (Mpayenda). When I got to the hospital room with my sons, we were met with elated smiles and joy. I needed to sit down as my legs were exhausted. I was approached by my brother Joshua who together with my sister Fida as well as his girlfriend ware with the baby girl. My sister Fida brought the little baby to me. I could see the special bond Fida, as the aunty, already had with the baby. Fida was emotional because she and Joshua were both young orphans when my parents adopted and brought them to the states and now Joshua is a dad!

CHAPTER 7

Dealing with Realities: Divorce Effects; Inability to Work; Continued Poor Healthy; Reflecting on My Life

My happiness was short-lived due to the continuing social instability I was experiencing. While the divorce was generally good for me because it would end the toxic relationship, there was another side to it, namely its impact on other aspects of my life. 'Baby' moved out of the house carrying with her practically whatever she could lay her hands on and leaving the house in a mess. This effect though, was not as devastating as the stress that was imposed by the pending divorce. Young as the boys were, one could still sense on the ongoing drama which involved constant yelling and having an empty house. The situation between 'baby' and I became so stressful that with the help of my sister Monica I filed an order of protection against her and it was granted.

Faced with all these challenges in general and my poor health in particular, it was practically impossible to request to work full time at the job I had. This in turn meant that my financial situation worsened as I could not pay all my bills. My family continued to generously support me, but for the sake of getting a long-time solution, my sister Monica emphasized social security disability. Thus in later 2011, with the help of Monica we collected all the required documents and applied for social security disability. To my surprise and many others, my social security application was denied because I made $50:00 above what the Federal Government required applicants to comply with.

Although my application was denied, I was now talking out loud and in a comfortable environment about the extreme physical and mental trauma that came with both of my ailments. I remembered how perplexed I was as on how a 'medical doctor' I trusted basically watched me almost die of celiac disease but insisted that it was just a tricky 'viral infection'. How could I let this happen to me, I angrily thought? But then I remembered how subtle this doctor's medical treatment was toward me and how desperate I was for answers as I was dying. I got emotional as my PTSD stirred within me. I felt lied to by the 'viral infection juggernaut'! But what could I do at this point, I thought? And what could I do about this? I further thought to myself. I recollected how negatively this all affected my job performance at the insurance company as my body was in pain and discomfort non-stop.

I very seriously thought about contacting an attorney about this doctor. But I realized I had two major obstacles at this point: First I had not seen him for several years: Secondly, I could not engage or be in lawsuit while in my current separation, per the contract with my divorce attorney. I did not let these obstacles prevent me from making phone calls to law offices about questionable medical practices. After speaking to a few attorneys, I quickly realized that I was not the only person to have dealt with such problems. Unfortunately I quickly discovered from the attorneys that I let too much time elapse. Even though these attorneys told me that too much time had elapsed for my medical questions I felt a sense of accomplishment by speaking out loud to an attorney.

I felt like life and hope was returning to me at this point. But my family members and I were taken aback what I needed to do with my denial from social security being it I was basically a lemon. But like a good advocate, Monica immediately noted that she had been told that an overwhelming majority of applications are denied on the first submission and this meant we needed to appeal. She further noted that since my denial was income-based, I had to leave my current job all together. Indeed, I could see my parents were perplexed as work is what they knew; but they nonetheless followed her lead. I was naturally troubled by the idea of leaving my job. However, Moni reiterated my need to leave my part-time job as the first order of business to start the appeal process. Consequently, I submitted my resignation in 2012.

I felt empty, abandoned and ashamed after I left the company headquarters and hobbled to my car. I immediately remembered how I was also limping after I left the first two companies after I lost those jobs. I regretfully recalled the false hope that I had in me at those respective times as my health declined. Even with my sickness compounding I regretfully remembered how I thought I was moving on to something better after leaving those secure jobs. It now dawned on me that part of the hope I should have had after leaving those jobs is the disability benefits I had paid for and was now currently seeking to attain with my sister Monica at the helm. I also regretfully realized that I would have been immediately approved for these benefits if I had filed for them right after my workplace injuries at those jobs as opposed to this tedious process I was currently going through.

With my PTSD acting up, I remembered all the money I was faithfully paying for those benefits! I then confusingly asked myself why I did not pursue these benefits I was entitled to? I then shamefully remembered how I did not follow up with the doctor, who diagnosed me with the celiac allergy in the 11th hour! I knew I was traumatized by the failed treatment I received up to then. I knew I was not healthy after that discharge with a gluten allergy diagnose and if I would've gone back in march of '03, they probably would've figured out the MS I was now dealing at that time. These thoughts made me tired! With these thoughts, I recalled how emotionally and physically fatigued I was and even now am just thinking about. Specifically, I was mentally and physically fatigued primarily from the doctor's 'viral' treatment, and I did not want any further medical treatment.

I again shamefully recollected how I had superb insurance with one of my previous companies and I had access to above average medical technology. I think they would have found the MS in me at that time, like a food allergy I had eaten all my life!. With the food allergy, I think they would have investigated the long-term ramifications of an illness like this waiting dormant on my body for so long in my life! Specifically, the main questions I personally had at the time was why such an allergy would manifest itself in me at 29 years of age and how was I dealing with it? I also think they would have found the lesions in my brain and MS with more tests also. I felt beguiled and totally wronged! With these troubling thoughts I struggled to keep my head up. But I kept a smile on my face to hide the pain. I did this because I had a fighting and overcoming spirit in me like my mom and dad at this point knowing that things would work out.

I reflected on these matters as I sat in my car in the parking lot. But I also remembered all the demands in my life at the present point in my life. Most importantly, I was concerned about the overall and general future well-being of my two sons God had blessed me with. I kept asking myself whether I would be able to keep up with the payment on the mortgage on my house and meet their emotional needs as boys growing up in this country. I remembered how I looked forward to these days when I was in graduate school just a few years back! My dreams were just beginning! I then remembered how I soon found solace and learned so much about myself as I made money working in real estate. I also remembered at this time how much I loved helping people and learning about their languages. I knew I was not healthy at this time because of my sickly episodes; but sharing these life events with my boys as they grew up I knew could help them as they found out what they wanted to do. But I felt remorse as I though that my inability to act on my entitled benefits could cost them!

As I was thinking out loud in my car, I asked myself why I did not reach out to an attorney throughout these medical and legal episodes I was receiving! I thought out loud to myself like when I broke my arm. Now that I officially was not working because of my MS injury I began to feel the same kind of aggrieved emotions like that of my broken arm. I signed a severance package with one of my major employers nine years ago and so I knew I had no recourse. Without an advocate at that time I remembered how I hurriedly signed severance forms from the company I loved working for. With this remorse, I continued evaluating my life in the last couple of years.

As I placed the key in the ignition, I immediately remembered my walk to my car when a doctor reluctantly gave me a referral to the hospital in February of 2003. I regret wasting my time telling one of the general doctors about my neurological problems. I wish, though, I had followed up on the referral one of the specialist doctor made for me. Why did I not consult with an attorney? Fortunately, I felt a sense of solace knowing that Monica, my advocate, had filed social security for me. I still could not help it but ask myself at the same time why this process did not start back at that moment in time when I worked for a major company and used to get so sick! How did I let almost nine years elapse since then, I shamefully thought? I felt beguiled and depressed as these past before me. I tried to keep my head up and stay positive as I felt the gravity of my mistakes overtake me, at that point!

My blood began to boil within me as I sat in my car looking to drive home and realizing that I was now unemployed! To help my thoughts I listened to the relaxing sounds of the South African gospel choir to keep my mind on that sacrifice Jesus made at Calvary. But I did not know what exactly was in front of me. I also was not done processing what had just happened, either. I immediately thought about that dreadful day on June 8th, 2008 and my subsequent MS diagnoses. I thought about how a doctor told me that MS was a traumatic injury to the brain. I knew that unlike my broken arm from years earlier I could not see this injury in plain sight like celiac. I could not even feel the pain like when my arm snapped into two pieces, save the nagging in my body, which I thought was something else. With MS the MRI showed that there were lesions in my brain adversely affecting my walking, writing, thinking and basically functioning like when I broke my arm. My heart started racing in me screaming foul! I knew my only consolation in all this, is that I now could now reflect on the past because of my sister Monica's guidance and advocacy.

With this train of thought, I began thinking about the legal recourse for me since my MS discovery was part of my workplace injury four years past. I also considered the shady business processes from the owner of the gold and silver shop and how he promised me benefits after ninety days that did not exist. I, though, realized that time was not on my side. I tried not to disqualify myself, nonetheless, because I was not an attorney. I continued wondering why I did not speak with an attorney at the time of the incident! I remembered meeting with WCCO and KMSP news representatives right after my injury. But then I recalled my inability to open up to them about what happened to me because of all the trauma from the accident. I thought it was all a bad dream! Lawyers would have most probably contacted me if I had told them about my accident and they would have helped me to resolve some of the issues I now faced.

I sat alone in my vehicle ready to depart and I realized this may have looked like I was day dreaming; but it was more of a nightmare! I had stay positive as my story was not done. I reminded myself how fortunate I was when Monica helped me obtain the insurance I desperately needed when my fortune was all but gone. As I inhaled in gratitude for my blessings and then I realized how much personal injury there was with me, as I exhaled! My heart began to sink as I realized I would have most definitely have recovered a substantial sum of money for my personal injury damages from these companies I worked for and a possible medical malpractice recovery! Instead, all of my hope at this stage was in a modest social security payment.

I proceeded to start my car and drive home. My skepticism overtook me since I was not sure about my poor timing as I kept driving away from the company headquarters. My thoughts got confusingly negative as to why I did not do anything for so long after either of my work place injuries. How did I do this to myself! Again, I immediately remembered the chilling words of a doctor telling me of my near fatal injury to my colon! I also recalled the sobering dictate of another doctor telling me that I had MS which is caused by an intricate injury to the brain. But I could not stop thinking of my ill-advised drive to the hospital with an unknown virus and in a delicate state I was in healthy-wise. I also recall during that drive to the hospital how I heard the angels talking to me through my gospel music when I wanted to take a nap en route to the hospital in 2003. Tears began to run down my eyes simultaneously as I heard the coloreds from South Africa singing 'Heaven is my home'. I realized that God was showing me mercy and giving me time! I drove into my nice neighborhood with tears running down my face.

Despite my heavy spirit, I began to settle down as I approached my house. Before I drove into my garage, I first stopped to check the mail. When I opened the mail box, I noticed a letter that was from my mortgage service that looked rather odd. I gave it top priority since I was curious to read it. I opened it and found out they were requesting a final mortgage payment. The first thing that caught my attention was a colossal amount showed at the top that they said I owed. As my tears dried, I read the letter that said I would have to pay the arrears immediately or they would begin the foreclosure process in sixty days. I knew that this would have to eventually take place. This fool's paradise I was living in with my deteriorating MS was relentless and quickly coming to an end. Therefore, I knew that barring a financial miracle from God I would not be able to pay the required amount and obtain finances to fix what was broken. As I read this letter, my emotions again stirred up within in me as I thought out loud and realized that all these current problems were work related from my injury at The telecommunications office on June 8, 2008 as my fatigue overwhelmed me. This feeling prompted me to conclude that I needed to seek the advice of an attorney with regard to that injury which happened four years ago!

Adrenaline was going through my body as I entered my house. Although I was beside myself, I felt relieved that I did not have to face a threatening environment with a woman on her phone and ready to fight. Thus, I turned on the TV and tried to rest on my sofa. As I flipped over the TV channels, most of the advertisements that came up were from attorneys for injuries of any type including workplace. I was ashamed that it took me so long to realize that I needed to speak with these legal advocates! I still felt ashamed to think they were talking to people like me. I was fatigued but I could not sleep because all I was thinking was my legal recourse since I could not now work because of my injury that happened years back. I decided to call one of the attorneys who was adverting. Fortunately, the attorney I called was receptive and sympathetic to my problems namely: my injury from The telecommunications company on June 8th, 2008; the ensuing hospitalization coupled with my MS diagnoses and then The telecommunications company's inability to rehire me when I stepped away for one week leaving me uninsurable, I told him. He attentively listened to me, sympathized, took notes and asked questions. I was shaking as I explained to him what transpired with me. However, I realized I had to explain to him why I let four years elapse! I thus hesitated to tell him the details of the whole story. As I further spoke to him, I remembered how I foolishly thought that time would have lessened all my physical and emotional pain. Now that I was speaking to a legal advocate about my injury, I could truly realize how traumatizing this event was for me. It seemed like it was yesterday with all the pain associated with it.

These events also seemed to have deeper meanings to me as I spoke to this attorney. Again this was highly therapeutic for me to speak with this person as I realized he was the legal advocate I did not have throughout my work debacles. I thus gained more confidence as I was speaking to him and so I mentioned the lie I was told by the owner of the gold and silver shop to obtain insurance. At the end of our conversation, he said he was very interested in what I was explaining to him as he could detect civil liability throughout! Immediately I was therefore thinking about possible financial compensation for all my pain and suffering I had been through on my job. I was thankful that I was thinking out loud and that I was speaking out loud to someone else who could help me with the legality of the matter. He promised to call me back after cross checking some of the information I gave him.

Even though I was energized after speaking with this attorney, my heart still sank when he communicated to me about his limited knowledge about my case. I think part of my hope is that I felt good I did not feel like I had not done anything wrong to be where I was. However, I was not ready to sit around and wait for him to call me back as I felt that complacency was part of why I was my present situation. I therefore began to call different attorneys in hopes of getting immediate answers. They were all victims' rights attorneys and they all had compassion about what I told them and they all said I had a very strong case. To my dismay, all of these attorneys indicated after I told them the date of my accident that my statute of limitations had expired to file a claim.

I knew what to expect from the first attorney I was still waiting to hear back from. After my conversation with the three latter attorneys, the writing on the wall was clear. How did I manage to sit around and wait for so long, I thought to myself? At this point I was unable to work because of these injuries. I had secure employment and exceptional insurance, but I had no financial security even though these were all workplace injuries, I said to myself in disgust! I felt abandoned and lonely. I tried not to put my head down; I had to stay positive as I hoped without a doubt that the first attorney would not give me similar feedback.

Depression began to overtake me. I therefore went to the scriptures and read the Bible to keep my mind on the Lord Jesus and what He overcame to stay positive. As I was reading, I realized that I finished another iteration of reading my Bible. My emotions overtook me and tears subsequently began to run down my face uncontrollably. This was timely because I had a lot of pent up emotions. I prayed and cried out loud with tears running down my face thanking the Lord for allowing me to see the day I was in. I also began asking God for deliverance from my precarious situation overall. I was emotionally exhausted and so I asked for strength to be a strong father to my children. I began to ask God how I got into my current situation as I felt I let them down with my workplace injuries with nothing to show for myself. Fortunately, I now knew I had a traumatic brain injury named MS thanks to informed, doctors. My boys at this point were also growing up fast and asking me questions as to why things were as they saw them. They saw their uncles, aunties and grandparents were healthy and successful. They saw how they had nice things and were all educated as I was. They had young cousins like them who were enjoying the benefits of their parents' hard work. They now would see me not working consistently and struggling to move in addition to struggling to move around, I thought. Their love and support was unconditional. But I knew they needed more answers than I am just sick or not feeling well! I knew their mom had been feeding them propaganda as to why I was not working full time like their uncles, aunties and grandparents. Regardless of that reasoning I still blamed myself for not saying anything to anyone throughout my medical collapse, despite my MS diagnoses, as my depression ensued.

My thoughts were spiraling downward as I thought about my medical and personal mishaps. I knew I had to look ahead with my head up as I could not turn back time. My tears subsequently began to dry as I relaxed on my couch. To keep my thoughts occupied, I turned on the TV and listened to CNN news. To my surprise, the program I listened to focused on the plight of people in Africa with regard to lack of getting access to medical treatment. I immediately started finding many similarities between the fight of these people for medical relevance and attention and my own situation as I thought out loud to myself. I realized that I would have just vanished and silently become irrelevant without an advocate or outside help much like these people. I also realized that as unique and complex as my situation was, that I was probably not the first person to suffer from this type of situation.

I slept for roughly three hours, but I was still worn out when I woke up from this nap. As I sat up, I felt disoriented and confused because I thought I should be at work. I then suddenly heard the doorbell ringing rapidly and my boys talking outside. I stood up to open the door straightaway, but I looked for where I could catch myself in case I fell. I opened the door and their energy gave me life. My mind was also reinvigorated. They brought therapy to me as I was fighting not to fall into a depression.

Now that my body was not in work mode and I was resting, my physical ailments began to become more apparent to me. My limping and stiffness and general fatigue specifically became more apparent to me as I gingerly moved to the kitchen or the restroom. Despite my MS diagnosis I still thought I was somehow doing something wrong, to exacerbate my situation like my food choices or exercise. I also naively kept my hopes in work mode. I was grateful that Lydia researched and realized the gravity of this sickness.

Fortunately, I heard my boys running around and making noise in the background as they came home from playing outside with their friends. Their energy and innocence made me feel guilty. The reason for this is I knew I could not sustain my lifestyle providing for the life they now had. Essentially, I had a nice looking home (from the outside) in a nice neighborhood that would not be there for me in six months, per the letter in my hand. My anxiety stressed me out as I did not know where I would live thereafter or how I would meet their needs as a father as they were getting older and asking me more questions! On that note, I did not know how I would explain everything to them about what happened to me, I shamefully thought? I also remembered my thoughts of the "Nekemiah's Empire" I had after I left Ghana in 1997 when all those children became my pen pals. Could I explain my dreams to them at this point if I was homeless or could not provide for myself?

My debilitating thoughts began to subside as I heard my boys calling out to me as they were looking for something to eat. Their voices put me in the here and now. Their youthfulness helped me to keep my mind preoccupied on thoughts of hope and positivity. But the negativity and depression in me kept reoccurring and intensifying. These debilitating thoughts intensified as I knew the family reunion at which my dad's 70th birthday celebration in July 2012 was approaching. I thought of what I would say to everyone since everyone in the family was generally successful. How would I explain to anyone about what was going on in my life or why I was limping and dragging my feet helplessly when I walked? All the thinking and wondering only made me more worried, anxious and depressed.

It was July of 2012 and the day of the event was finally at hand. Everything was at a location at one of the state universities. My boys were excited to be with their cousins. But I was very nervous as I rehearsed what I would say to anyone if I was asked what was going on in with my life and work. But to avoid many of these problems I would look for Lydia and stay as close to her and follow her lead. The intensity and thought of seeing everyone still immediately brought jitters to me and therefore I smiled to give the impression that I had everything under control.

As I showed up at the event with my boys, my focus was on not tripping and falling as I moved around. I did not want to use a walker even though I was previously advised to bring it. Basically, I did not want to answer any questions from anyone as to what happened to me if I used my walker; but I also did not want to answer questions as to why I was limping since this was a work place injury. I therefore chose to gingerly walk with a limp and balance myself with any objects in my path. As I hobbled along, I saw many people who looked at me awkwardly as my limp was obvious. I just smiled like it was a pulled muscle or nothing serious. My heart dropped when I saw friends that I went to school with who also saw me limping around with my two children without their mother.

Even though I recognized many faces there, I felt lonely as I hobbled and sat down with my boys. I immediately observed my surroundings to see where restrooms were and strategized what I would catch myself on. My boys saw their cousins and immediately joined them. I saw my parents greeting everyone as they were the reason for our gathering. I then saw Monica seated by them and so I sat next to her and reevaluated the surroundings around me. I felt comfortable as I sat next to Lydia because she had everything under control in my life. But I still felt ashamed that I was not working as everyone there was a success and hard work story as she was. What made this even more stressful for me, is that I had no income even though my injuries were both work related. I just kept quiet, smiled and followed her orders.

Overall, I enjoyed attending this event because I was able to connect up with my family and friends. Despite this special enjoyment and excitement, I was nervous to interact with many people who were educated and had good jobs. Indeed, it was frustrating to realize that I would be moving up in my career like everyone who came to the party if it were not for my sicknesses! I felt that the most trying moment of the occasion this evening was when family members stood before the masses to give personal testimonies as they related to our parents and I could only sit down without an explanation to all who remembered a healthy graduate student a few years back.

Specifically, we situated in the front of the masses and began giving our personal testimonials. I sat on the chair as my siblings stood up. We then proceeded to introduce ourselves and our relation to my parents. We were all emotional as we spoke since we realized the magnitude of the phenomenon that we were in. Everyone was standing as they spoke except me. As the microphone was passed to me, I quickly gave a brief testimony. I, though, immediately felt awkward as I was speaking. Sitting down as my siblings were standing up made me feel like I owed everyone an explanation. Indeed, I had a story to tell and a testimony to give as I had started to actually deal with my problems. I wanted to tell everyone what has happened to me. But time and opportunity would not afford me at this juncture. I just said thanks and kept quiet.

After giving our testimonials, we next prepared for dinner, in the next ten minutes. Nature was calling me at this point and I had to use the restroom. Everyone was standing, stretching out and preparing for the meal. I strategized how I would make it to the restroom. I therefore put my head down and analyzed the ground to make sure nothing would trip me up. I knew tripping and falling would bring attention to me and I would have to explain to everyone my situation. Although I was ready to explain to all what had happened to me the timing was not right at this point. I thus continued analyzing my walkway by looking for furniture that I could lean on as I would traverse. Finally, I looked around to see who was watching before I started. It seemed that everyone was distracted and so I began moving.

As I began walking, I could feel attention focusing on me. Regardless of this fact I kept moving. I felt my right leg helplessly dragging on the ground as I was walking. I had accepted this situation as the norm at this point with this MS. Specifically I had started dealing with this part of the disease of my MS since my collapse on June 8th, 2008. I successfully made it to the bathroom. After exiting the restroom, I ran into a family friend Kwesi from Ghana. I felt comfortable around him. He knew me and my family from my youth as my parents mentored him in the 1980's as a student at A local university where my parents worked. When he saw me, he ended his cell phone call and talked to me. He saw me leaning on the wall as I looked disoriented and he probably realized for the first time how MS is negatively impacting my life.

After dinner we were ready to go home. Metaphorically, I exhaled with a sigh of relief. Indeed, I enjoyed seeing everyone but my façade was wearing off. I was also getting fatigued and I wanted to rest. All of my contemporaries had finally seen me and I was ready to go back to my silence and obscurity. I did my best to act disinterested in all matters and discussions as I waited to leave. To numb the pain and discomfort, I did not spend time or catch up with anyone as my shame and fatigue simultaneously increased. I therefore timidly sat by my sister Monica and thought to myself out loud. The reality of doing nothing with all the education I have bothered me as the party ended.

I, though, kept cool and nervously smiled as I began to walk out with my boys. I had to look down as I limped to make sure nothing would trip me up. Putting my head down as I hobbled reminded me how depressed I really was. I needed to stay strong for my boys, I told myself. They immediately told me how much fun they had and how they wanted to have another get together like this one. They were also asking questions about people they met at the event. I knew they were connecting the dots as they probably knew education and success was a big part of their paternal story. I did my best to keep the attention off of me. But I know I needed to answer them as they would probably want to know more specifically why and how things are with me today. I also knew I would need to provide answers to everyone who knew my plight and accomplishments more closely, especially family and friends. In the meantime, I wanted to be alone and think out loud as I was getting depressed the more I thought about the reality of what was in front of me.

Things would get more uncertain for me in subsequent days as to my next course of action was to hurry up and wait for social security to hopefully approve my appeal. These days became difficult and stressful as I could barely move my body with all the stress in my life. Regardless of this reality, we were all still frustrated that my initial disability was declined because I only made a few dollars too much. This whole process was uncharted territory. This stress of waiting was exacerbated as I would have to wait as I was living in an increasingly uninhabitable home that would be redeemed in February of 2013. Additionally, I had no place to go and I did not have any income to plan for my move. My anxiety increased uncontrollably as my confusion would turn into tears as I began tending to my physical problems. I confusingly could not think of my MS as a true disability because social security did not approve it. I kept smiling outwardly and did my best to stay positive as I nervously waited to see what my next course of action would be.

Fortunately, my family also knew the pressure I felt. With Monica, as my advocate, knew I was diligently ready for my appeal. Monica's help was greatly appreciated in light of the fact that my parents had retired and live 70 miles away from my residence. As we approached August of 2012, I received news that Monica had taken a new appointment as assistant principal at a different high school. Although I was proud of her accomplishment, this reality brought troubling concerns to me as I thought she would not have any more time to help me with my issues. Basically, I knew the demands for this new role intensified her work responsibilities as her demands for her own children also were increasing. Regardless of these pressures, she kept treating my issues with high importance. Most importantly she kept on planning on my new reality living with MS, as the debilitating disease that it is. With my MS ailing me she still kept working on getting my social security appeal approved.

Despite Monica's keen interest in this appeal, we were advised by people who have dealt with situations similar to ours that involving an attorney on the appeal process would quicken the process. Consequently, Monica put all the documents together and handed them to an attorney who was methodical and thorough. The attorney confessed that he did not need to work hard since Monica had practically done all that was needed. In other words, all he did was to attach his name to the documents Monica prepared and sent them for appeal consideration.

Although the approval in my social security disability was welcome news in that it somewhat eased my financial challenges, the road ahead of me was full of new problems. First the limited funds I get, some of it had to be given to my boys who do not live with me. To complicate matters, due to my sickness I am not in a position to get a part-time job to supplement the funds I get from social security. In other words, I still have to depend on my family for my daily expenses. The family support was particularly critical between April 2011 when I first submitted my social security disability application. Their support continued through January 2013 when it was finally approved which coincidentally marked 10 years after my sicknesses I got in 2003.

CHAPTER 8

Concluding Remarks: My Story in a Nutshell, Lessons Learned

This is my story of a young man who was born in Uganda on February 4, 1974, but migrated to the USA with the rest of my family. I completed High School, received a Bachelor of Arts (BA), and pursued a graduate degree in Business Administration (MBA). Endowed with excellent qualifications and upbringing, job opportunities were open for me and the as the saying is always made – "The Sky is the limit". Yes, I was offered decent jobs but all this came to a standstill when in June 2008 I was diagnosed with MS. The devastating impact of MS made it practically impossible for me to perform as I was expected, consequently making me lose one job after another.

The loss of income meant that I became economically destitute and yet I have a family to support. Indeed, my family came to my rescue, but the bottom line was that I needed a constant income to supplement whatever partial financial help I was getting. My brief successful participation in the mortgage industry was cut short by the outbreak of 2008 recession. Due to my denial about having MS and reluctance to get an advocate to advise me about what transpired on June 8, of 2008, I did not apply for social security disability assistance until April 2011.

In addition to MS and my never ending economic woes, my situation was worsened by getting involved into an ill-advised social relationship with a girl I did not know, but who gave birth to my two beautiful sons I now regard as my supporters. However, my home became toxic since there was daily bickering about everything on the planet. As one would expect, such environment was neither good for my boys nor for myself. This notwithstanding, I point out that I probably would have weathered most of the challenges if it were not for my being afflicted by the devastating effects of MS.

Faced with all these challenges I was shocked and at the same time skeptical when in 2012 my parents suggested that for the sake of providing a record for my boys, I should start working on my autobiography. Aside from the fact that the idea was outlandish given that an autobiography is usually written at the end one's career, I was not particularly excited about the idea of searching around for the information about the past. Besides I was discouraged by the lack of interest by other members of the family in such a project due to their full time work schedules. However, my parents persistently reminded me about my plight and the need for me to chronicle events in my life which if I did not do, could be lost in obscurity. I thus concluded that the act of recording everything in my life would probably be therapeutic and comforting.

Once I started researching and writing down my thoughts, it became clear that there are important lessons that can be learned from my personal experience. Seeking and listening to other people's advice is one thing I lacked. Probably if I had carefully listened and assessed the advice of many people who cautioned me about getting involved with a girl I practically knew nothing about my social life would have been different! But again, I thank God for the beautiful children He gave to me too through her. Indeed, I had poor social relationship in my home that negatively impacted me in everything. At a time when I needed help, what I got instead were curses and insults that made it difficult for me to think clearly.

But I also failed to open up to the news men who visited me where I was working to look into how I was treated when I fell ill on June 8,

2008. As I document in the chapters above, I did not get immediate medical attention and that could have been considered as being negligent on part of the employer. Probably, there could have been financial compensation for me if this matter was taken up to court particularly given that this is a company I had worked for over three years! I also note that this company would have been exposed for lack of remorse because they refused to rehire me a week after I stepped away. The negative news exposure would thus be beneficial for me personally, but it will also be educational for the community at large.

I also feel that my situation would have been much better if instead of taking up any job that looked promising, I first sought the advice of others who had some experience before making such decisions. By not doing this, I made the ill-fated decision to leave a god job for another company whose pay seemed high, but was physically exerting while I was suffering from MS. This was a bad decision because I lost the great medical benefits the company had and brought myself into a pernicious market with a pre-existing condition. I blame some companies for the poor medical services I received. The truth of the matter though, I should own part of this blame because of my failure to take up the good advice I was given by some doctors for follow up on checkups. Yes, indeed there is no cure for MS, but an early diagnosis is supposed to slow down the process of the disease. Consequently, I have paid dearly for my inability to do what I was required to do.

The centrality of my family in my life is another good example of lessons learned. I have noted in many parts of the book how my family, in spite of my failure to seek and listen to the advice they gave me, has been generous to me both financially and socially. The case in point was when my family put up a fund to assist me when I became unemployed. They have continued giving me their support even after the approval of my social security disability. I will forever be grateful for their generosity particularly in the light of the fact that they have their own personal challenges they face.

I also appreciate greatly the generosity of Aunt Matilda and Uncle Noah Ivule for providing a social venue for my boys and myself. Practically every Sunday after church my boys and I visit their home.

This get together gives us an opportunity to eat homemade food, but more importantly allows us to interact with other members of the family. This is indeed refreshing because it enables me to get out of my cocoon. Frankly I hate to admit that if I did not have the family support, I would probably become homeless with my workplace injuries.

My sister Monica has gone beyond the call of duty by becoming my advocate. She has been there for me since my illness became overwhelming. Among the many things she had done for me include, but not limited to: completing various applications for housing, social disability, heating bills, medication, children summer programs for my boys, to name a few. What is remarkable about Monica is that she finds time to do all this for me despite having a hectic schedule for her work and family.

Lastly, my parents have sacrificed their meagre retirement income to help me with my various bills since my disability funds cannot cover all the bills. What further complicates my situation is that I am not in a position to work at all. They just not help out with bills but they provide me with home cooked meals when they drive down the 70 miles journey to come and help me clean the apartment. What this means for me is that I just do not have caring parents but I am also dearly loved.

My church is central in my life. In addition to giving me spiritual support, my church also provides a social venue through which I can interact with church members. Yes, indeed most of my family members live near me, but due to their hectic schedules, I usually see them over the weekends particularly when there is a social function like birthdays or holiday weekends. The church therefore fills up this void. Consequently, I look forward to going to church on Sundays and Wednesdays. I was greatly elated when I was appointed Associate Minister in my church (an Apostolic Church in the cities). Although there is hardly any monetary reward attached to this position, I consider this appointment as monumental in my life because in spite of my ill health they felt confident enough to offer me the appointment. I still unfairly blame myself for many things that were out of my control and that would've probably been rectified speedily if I would've stayed on course and lawyered up (when needed), as they say. But I now know that trauma also distorts reality as our wounds need to heal at the same time. In hindsight at the end of the day, I know that we all also have a story of our own to tell. This story concludes mine, and is now my American Dream, and so I ask, what is yours?

CPSIA information can be obtained
at www.ICGtesting.com
Printed in the USA
JSHW081232120623
43031JS00002B/88